Rev. Andrew Broaddus.

A HISTORY

OF THE

Broaddus Family,

From the Time of the Settlement of the
Progenitor of the Family in the
United States down to
the year 1888.

———

BY A. BROADDUS, D. D.,

OF SPARTA, VA.,

WITH AN INTRODUCTION BY JOHN A. BROADUS, D.D.,

LOUISVILLE, KY.

Another Quality Reprint of a Classic Book
by

The Apple Manor Press

Markham, Virginia

2016

Thousands of titles available at:
www.AppleManorPress.com

ISBN 13: 978-1-5421-0000-7

A HISTORY

OF THE

Broaddus Family,

From the Time of the Settlement of the
Progenitor of the Family in the
United States down to
the year 1888.

BY A. BROADDUS, D. D.,

OF SPARTA, VA.,

WITH AN INTRODUCTION BY JOHN A. BROADUS, D.D.,

LOUISVILLE, KY.

ST. LOUIS :
CENTRAL BAPTIST PRINT,
1109 OLIVE STREET

PREFACE.

The author of this history has written it at the request of friends in whose judgment he confides, and with whose wishes he has felt desirous to comply. But even these considerations would hardly have induced him to enter on an undertaking so beset with perplexities and difficulties had these been fully anticipated. It has been no easy task to straighten out the tangled skein of relationship between the members of a family so numerous and so widely scattered as that of which this history treats. After all his efforts in this direction, the author is well aware that he has met with but indifferent success. Never having seen a treatise on heraldry, and having no acquaintance with the principles (if there be any) on which genealogical trees are constructed, the author has been at a loss to fix on the best plan for tracing the lineage of the members of the family with which he has had to do. After some hesitation he determined to take the children of the first person of the name of whom anything is known, in the order of their ages, and to trace the descendants of each as far as these have been ascertained. That is, after following down the line of the oldest child as far as it could be traced, then to return and take the next oldest, and so on. This appeared to be the most natural and the least objectionable plan.

The genealogical chapters even of the Bible are very
dry reading, and a similar array of names in any other
book must be even less interesting. The author has tried
to break the monotony of such dull reading, in the present
volume, by recording incidents of family history which
seem to have some interest, and by efforts at the delineation of character. The extent to which he has succeeded
must, of necessity, be left to the judgment of the reader.

Possibly it may be objected by some that, in this
history, disproportionate space has been given, by the
author, to the members of his immediate family, and to
his intimate acquaintances. To any such objection the
answer is. that the author must, of necessity, have said
most concerning those of whom he knew most, and that
he has gladly rec. ived and freely used information from
any quarter, and in regard to any member of the family.

The facts stated in regard to the early history of the
Broaddus family were derived from an account written
more than half a century ago by Judge A. S. Broaddus,
now of Texas, from the dictation of his mother, then an
old woman. These statements, I have no doubt, are in
the main correct, as they came from an intelligent lady
who had good opportunity to know whereof she affirmed.
In addition to the information derived from Judge Broaddus' record the writer is indebted for sketches of their
respective families to Andrew Broaddus, of Louisville,
Ky., Rev. W. A. Gaines, of South Carolina, Wm. O.
Broaddus, of Arkansas, Judge Elbridge J. Broaddus, of
Missouri, Wm. H. C. Broaddus, of Arkansas, Dr. Thomas
E. Broaddus, of Missouri. Miss Lavinia Broadus, of
Charlestown, W. Va.; Dr. John A. Broadus, of Louis-

ville, Ky., and Hon. Andrew Broaddus, of Luray, Va.; and he is under special obligations to Rev. M. E. Broaddus, of Clinton, Mo., for the interest he has manifested in the preparation of this work, and for his active efforts in obtaining materials. He has also had charge of the publication of the same.

It will be seen by those who shall read this little volume with any attention, that there are several branches of the Broaddus family whose lineage the author has been unable to trace; so that even in this respect it is an imperfect history. But in spite of these drawbacks it is committed to the hands of the printer with the hope that at least some who read it may find in its pages matter of entertainment, and perhaps even of profit.   A. B.

Sparta, Va., Feb. 13, 1888.

INTRODUCTION.

It is time to cease calling ours a new country. In the Atlantic States there has long been something of that interest in history which is one characteristic of older communities. Centennial celebrations have of late been spreading into Kentucky and Ohio, and cannot fail to promote historical inquiry. An humble, but quite important department of such inquiry is into the history of families. In the States immediately west from Virginia, one often meets persons who will say, "My father- or, my grandfather—came from Virginia." Yet they will frequently not know from what county in Virginia, and very seldom know anything of their kindred now living in the Old Dominion. In the Atlantic States it is not uncommon to find a family which has continued to be largely represented in the same general locality for a century or even two centuries. If any person of such a family connection became widely known, those who moved westward often retained the memory of their kinship to him; and this makes it possible to gather a somewhat complete family history. Thus very nearly all persons throughout the South and West who bear the name of Broaddus are aware of being akin to the famous Rev. Andrew Broaddus, of Virginia. In my own boyhood it was a great delight to make a long journey on horse-

back to one and another "Association," which it was reported that this venerable man would attend; and no little pride was felt in being even remotely akin to one so
famous and so gifted. Even those branches of the family
which it has not been possible to trace in collecting
material for this volume would doubtless be found,
wherever they exist, to maintain the same recollection,
often attesting it by the use of the name Andrew.

A son of this central person in the family history has
continued to live in the home of his ancestors, and has
been personally well acquainted with the wide circle of
families having the same blood in that part of Eastern
Virginia. It is an occasion of gratitude that he has been
spared to prepare this work, as no one else would have
been nearly so well qualified for the task.

If any person of some other family who may glance at
these pages should feel the desire to obtain a similar
history, it may be suggested that he must look to the
older States for materials, and in general for persons
cherishing the requisite interest in the undertaking.

For the practical enterprise of securing and publishing
this family history, those concerned are entirely indebted to Rev. M. E. Broaddus, whose zealous and efficient
exertions deserve our hearty gratitude. As the demand
for such a volume cannot in the nature of things be large,
it is suggested that all members of the family connection
who can afford to do so shall procure several copies. Why
should not a father give one to each of his children,
writing the name in the book, with a charge to preserve
it carefully and hand it down to future generations? If
such family histories were numerous and many copies

preserved, the future difficulty of preparing works of general history would be greatly lessened.

It is likely that all persons of the Broaddus name or blood who may look through this volume will feel somewhat more closely drawn together, and perhaps take some pleasure in thinking of kindred far remote from themselves in time or place. And it may not be amiss to offer the respectful suggestion that in every household this might be made the occasion of wholesome exhortation. Noble men and lovely women will be found mentioned, most of them all too briefly, on the successive pages of this little volume. Teach your children that these are their kindred; and that they themselves must beware of being the first to disgrace the name, and must strive to be not the least in bearing it worthily and giving it further claims upon the general respect. Let us all endeavor to rear our families in the highest possible intelligence and moral preparation for usefulness, in the fear of God and the Christian's immortal hope; and so to pursue our individual lives that those who come after shall feel at least no shame in being our kindred.

The author of this volume, Dr. A. Broaddus, naturally abstained from saying much about himself, while speaking in the most generous eulogy of his kinsfolk. It has been suggested that the desire which will doubtless be felt by the whole family connection to know more concerning him might be partly gratified by a brief account in this Introduction, which will not pass under his eye.

Andrew Broaddus, Junior (known during his father's life and long afterwards as Andrew Ju.) was born in Caroline County, Va. After attending various neighborhood schools and then the Rappahannock Academy, a boarding school of high grade, he went first to the Richmond Seminary (now Richmond College), and afterwards to the Columbian College (now Columbian University) in Washington City. After an early marriage he purchased a farm near the village of Sparta, which has ever since been his home.

It was not till the age of 28 that he made a profession of religion, and being baptized by Rev. R. W. Cole, joined the Salem Church. He soon commenced speaking in public, before long was ordained, and for several years was pastor of Carmel and Bethesda Churches in Caroline. When his father died in 1848, he was called to Salem and Upper King and Queen Churches, of which he has ever since been pastor.

It was matter of early and frequent remark that Andrew Ju. was quite unlike his father. The one had been rich in all delicate and beautiful fancies and charming sentiments, and remarkable for suavity and grace, and for shrinking sensitiveness. The other was thoroughly practical, self-reliant and straightforward. It is quite possible that a natural feeling of independence led him by choice to pursue lines of exertion and self-development as unlike his father as possible. For often, when he would allow himself the chance or would be carried away by his theme, he has shown, at least for some passing moment, a power of imagination, a wealth of tender feeling, and always an unconquerable preference for the re-

---

tiring life of a country pastor, which vividly recalled notable traits in his honored father. Dr. Broaddus is a man of unusual strength of character, of decided convictions and high moral courage. He seems to revel in the sharp conflicts of high debate, especially where he is in a minority, or even seems to stand alone. Yet no man has a warmer or more affectionate heart. Not only his family, but various special friends have always been the objects of his most tender affection. His generous expenditure of time and money upon the afflicted and the needy has been in the highest degree remarkable ; and though always receiving a moderate salary he has given to general religious benevolence and local charities what would in the aggregate amount to large sums.

He possesses a rich store of varied and accurate information. In all the region where he lives his opinions are in constant demand, not only on religious points, but on business questions, on matters of law and medicine; and he has a great reputation as a peacemaker. He shows thorough knowledge and strong feelings in regard to political questions and leading public men of the past and the present.

As a speaker, Dr. Broaddus is deliberate, perspicuous, instructive and forcible. He never discusses any subject without leaving his hearers with clearer views in regard to it. In the pulpit his style is uniformly solemn and reverential. On the platform, he is sometimes highly humorous, and his speeches reveal the keenest wit, as also appears in his delightful conversation. His illustrations are drawn, without apparent effort, from the whole range of literature and history, as well as from the various occupations of men, and from the sciences, the mechanical arts, and the great book of nature. In the exposition of Scripture he is singularly clear and attractive. His articles in various periodicals are always vigorous, and often felicitous in a high degree. A beloved and successful pastor, an oracle among all the people of two counties, and respected throughout the State, Dr. Broaddus has lived a noble and honored life, which in tangible usefulness has probably even surpassed that of his distinguished father. JOHN A. BROADUS.

HISTORY.

Ancestral pride, when it induces self-respect, elevates above mean actions, and incites to worthy deeds, is praiseworthy. But to claim credit, or to assume airs of superiority on account of the character, the reputation, or the position of one's connections has as little support in right reason, as it has in the Scriptures, which teach that " every one shall give account of himself to God." If men may claim credit for the abilities displayed, the attainments reached, the distinction acquired, or the virtues practiced by

17

some of their relatives, it follows that they are responsible for the vices and misconduct of others; and, in such adjustment of accounts, the balance will often be found largely against the claimant. But while true honor cannot be conferred by the virtues, nor real disgrace inflicted by the vices of relatives, yet a desire to know something of those connected with us by ties of blood, and gratification in the assurance that some of them have deserved well of the community, are natural feelings, and if not commendable, are certainly not censurable. It is to meet this desire, and to gratify this feeling that the following history is written: for it is intended not for the general public, but for the family whose lineage and connection it records, and for any others who may feel a personal interest in that family.

There can be little question that the name Broaddus, was originally Broadhurst, contracted readily, first in pronunciation and afterwards in spelling, into Broaddus. There are now, in the United States, persons who wear the name Broadhurst, and the ancestors of these, I have little doubt, held in Wales (whence both the name and the family origi-nated) a common origin. a common name, and a family connection with the ancestors of the present Broaddus family of this country. On this point Dr. John A. Broadus writes: "The name Broaddus, according to a tradi-tion in the family, is a contraction of Broad-hurst. One of the family* found some years ago in London that whenever he gave his name to a shop-keeper or the like for sending home a package, it was without hesitation written Broadhurst. The name corresponds to Whitehurst, Deerhurst, Penhurst, Med-hurst, etc. The word Hurst alone is also a family name. It signifies a wooded hill or

* Dr. J. A. B. himself.

knoll, so that all the names of the group are primarily territorial. While the name is evidently Anglo-Saxon, it is a tradition that the family came from Wales. The late Professor Benjamin Davies, of Regent's Park College, London, explained this by stating that there has long been a considerable Anglo-Saxon settlement in South Wales. He once lived there and remembers the name Hurst as existing among them. It is certain that the family is not of properly Welsh, *i. e.*, Celtic origin, but is Anglo-Saxon. The name Broadhurst is frequently found in London, and Henry Broadhurst is now a member of Parliament, and was a member of Mr. Gladstone's last government. All who spell the name in the abridged form Broaddus, or Broadus, in all parts of our Southern and Western States, are found to be aware of kinship to the late Rev. Andrew Broaddus of Caroline county, Virginia."

The family name is written by a few members of the family with only one d, but by the great majority with two ds. This difference of spelling furnished occasion for the story of "the two ds," which the late Rev. Dr. Wm. F. Broaddus frequently told, and which, with his taste and talent for the humorous, he greatly enjoyed, though it was through his own oversight that the ludicrous mistake involved was made. This story is well known in Virginia, but as this history will probably fall into the hands of some who never heard it, it may not be amiss to relate it here.

At one time Dr. Broaddus was the pastor of the Baptist church in Fredericksburg, Va. During his pastorate a new church building was erected. After the house was finished the pews were sold and Dr. Broaddus bought one. Among the members of the church was a gentleman of taste and energy; and Dr. Broaddus commissioned this gentleman to purchase a plate, have his (Dr. B.'s) name engraved on it, and affix it to his pew. In giving instructions about the plate, Dr. Broaddus directed that only the surname, Broaddus, should be engraved on it, omitting the given name. He then added, "be sure and put in the two d's." Now it so happened that not long before this Columbian College had conferred on Dr. Broaddus the title Doctor of Divinity. After some time had elapsed, Dr. Broaddus noticed that the names of the owners had been affixed to nearly all the pews that had been sold while his pew remained nameless. Meeting with the gentleman who had been commissioned to have the plate prepared, Dr. B. inquired as to the cause of the delay. The gentleman seemed somewhat embarrassed, and said he did not think there was room on the plate for the two d's. Dr. Broaddus replied, "It is only one more letter and that is not a capital." "No," said the gentleman, "there are two letters and both are capitals." It then came out that the gentleman understood Dr. Broaddus as requesting that his new title, D. D., should be affixed to his name; and this the gentle man thought in such wretched taste, that he postponed having the plate engraved, with the hope that Dr. Broaddus would himself see the impropriety, not to say the absurdity of having "Broaddus, D. D.," engraved on his pew plate.

The difference in the spelling of the name Broaddus came about, according to the information of the present writer, in this wise. Some ninety or a hundred years ago, a member of the family went from Caroline county, Va., where at that time nearly all the Broadduses resided, to Culpeper county in the same State. After he married and settled in the last named county, all intercourse ceased between him and the members of the family in Caroline, and for convenience, or from some other cause, he dropped one d out of his name.* His spelling has been followed by very few, even of his own descendants, while all others of the name have retained the two d's. As an abstract question, I think the spelling with one d is to be preferred, because it is more in harmony with the supposed etymology of the name, accords better with the sound, and is more readily written. If there could be general concurrence in the change, by those wearing the name, the present writer would be very willing to drop one d from the middle of his name, and either with or without such concurrence, he would be equally willing to drop the two d's that have been tacked on to the end of it. In this history the name will be written as it is

---

*See below. Dr. John A. Broadus' account of the origin of the dif_ ference in the spelling of the family name. It differs from the account above given, and also from the account given by Dr. Wm. F. Broaddus: but seems to be the most probable.

spelled by those who wear it, the d being inserted or omitted according to the practice of the person mentioned, so far as that practice may be known to the writer.

But whether the name be spelled with one d, or with two d's, or whether it has been entirely changed by marriage for altogether another name, there has always been a disposition wherever any Broaddus blood existed, to "claim kin," however remote the relationship. To this disposition is, probably, due the fact that track has been kept, for more than a hundred and fifty years, of many branches of a family so numerous, and so widely scattered; and to the same disposition is to be attributed, I judge, the desire expressed by so many persons connected with the Broadduses, that a record should be made and preserved of the family lineage and history.

The first Broaddus of whom anything is

known—the progenitor of the family in the United States, was

EDWARD BROADDUS,

who emigrated from Wales and settled on Gwynn's Island, in Virginia. In Judge A. S. Broaddus' narrative Gwynn's Island is located in James River. This is evidently a mistake. There is no such island in James River. But there is a Gwynn's Island in the Piankitank River, in Matthews county, Va., near the junction of that river with the Rappahannock. It was there, doubtless, that Edward Broaddus first settled. It is not known in what year he emigrated from Wales, nor how long he remained on Gwynn's Island. From there he came in 1715, to the lower part of Caroline, then King and Queen county, Va., and purchased a farm on which he resided till his death, at about the age of seventy. He was twice married. The maiden name of his first wife is not known, nor is it known whether she came with him from Wales, or whether he married her after reaching the United States. His second wife was Mary Shipley, whom he married before coming to Caroline. By his first marriage Edward Broaddus had two sons, Thomas and Richard, and two or three daughters, the name of only one of whom, Dolly, is remembered. By his second marriage he had five sons, John, William, James, Shipley and Robin, and one daughter, Elizabeth. Edward Broaddus appears to have been a sober, plodding, laborious man, who, by industry and economy, accumulated sufficient property to give his children a start in the world.

Thomas Broaddus, oldest son of Edward, by his first marriage, like his father, spent his life in agricultural pursuits. He died suddenly at seventy years of age, never having removed from Caroline county. He was a soldier in the Revolutionary war. He married Ann Redd, by whom he had seven sons, Edward, Thomas, Shildrake, Mordecai, John, Richard and Redd, and four daughters, Catharine, Elizabeth, Ann and Sarah. His widow, Ann, was greatly respected by her acquaintances, and greatly beloved by her relatives, and died at the advanced age of ninety-six years.

The following record of his descent from the first Thomas Broaddus is furnished by Andrew Broaddus, of Louisville, Ky.; it also supplies the only account I have seen of any of the descendants of Robin Broaddus, the seventh son of the first settler. Andrew Broaddus says: "We are descendants of Thomas Broaddus, the first son of Edward, through my grandmother Elizabeth Motley, and of Robin, the seventh son of Edward, through my grandfather, William. The record is:

THOMAS BROADDUS

and

ANN REDD, his wife.

Children as follows:

Edward

Thomas

Shildrake

Mordecai

John

Redd

Catharine

Elizabeth

Ann

Sarah

CATHARINE BROADDUS

and

EDWIN MOTLEY.

Their children:

William

John

Richard

Elizabeth

Polly

and six others.

ROBERT- or ROBIN BROADDUS

and

SARAH HARWOOD, his wife.

Children as follows:

Warner	Mary
William	Caroline
Robert	America

The record of all but William is missing.

WILLIAM BROADDUS

and

ELIZABETH MOTLEY.

Their children :

Reuben	Betsy
Edwin	
Robert	
Warner	
William	
Mordecai	

REUBEN BROADDUS (1st son)

and

MARTHA LAVINIA OLIVER.

Their children :

William	Willintina
Robert Bruce	Martha Ellen
John	Mary Emily

Reuben   Virginia

Andrew   Catharine E.

EDWIN BROADDUS (2nd son)

and

ELIZA MONTAGUE.

Muscoe   Virginia

William   Betty

ROBERT BROADDUS (3rd son):

One child—name unknown.

Warner, 4th son, died at 19 years of age.

William, 5th son—no offspring.

Mordecai, 6th son—no offspring.

William Broaddus, son of Robin Broaddus and Sarah Harwood, with his wife, Elizabeth Motley, settled near Glenn's P. O., Gloucester county, Va. The house in which he lived was a substantial brick structure, the walls being two feet thick, with stair rails of solid walnut. It is still standing, being now occupied by the widow of William, son of Edwin

Broaddus. The house is now 147 years old. Reuben Broaddus, with his wife and three children, Robert B., John F. and Willintina, (Wm. L. died in infancy), emigrated to Cincinnati in 1831, and thence to Covington, Ky., in 1841. Of their children four, Reuben, Jr., Martha Ellen, Mary Emily and Andrew, were born in Cincinnati, and three, Virginia R., Mary Emily, (the first of this name died in infancy), and Catharine Emma, in Covington.

Reuben was a carpenter and builder, at which he was very successful. He was a member of the Baptist church from his youth —a man of strict integrity, and of the highest sense of honor. He was a kind, indulgent father, and a model husband; his wife, Martha, a gentle Christian woman. All their children, that reached the age of discretion, united with the Baptists, except Robert Bruce, who, although he always attended church, did not profess religion until a few years ago, when he joined the Presbyterian church, of which his wife was a member. He (R. Bruce), the oldest after William's death, married Harriet J. Wilson, of Kenton county, Ky., and has since then followed farming. He has had four children, Roderick, Emma, Tina and Addie. Emma, now dead, married Edward Bryson. Tina married Charles Poor, Roderick and Addie are unmarried, and live with their parents. John F. was a carpenter in his earlier years, but for several years prior to his death in 1860, he held the office of General Purchasing Agent of the Kentucky Central railroad. He married Adien Riggs, of Covington. He left one son, Charles, who is unmarried, and lives in Los Angeles, California. Reuben died in infancy. Andrew (the writer of this record) went into the Confederate army at 21 years of age, becoming a member of Co. I., 2nd Kentucky Cavalry,

Gen. Morgan's command, and continued in the service until the end of the war. Returning home, he remained in Covington a few months, and then became connected with the Louisville & Nashville Railroad, and now holds position as Assistant General Freight Agent of that Company's lines. He married Miss Mary Amelia Smith, of Louisville, by whom he had five children, Jessie, Mortimer, Bruce, Russel and Logan. His wife died in 1882, and he was again married in 1887, to Mrs. Frank Duncan Martin, of Nashville, Tenn. He is a deacon of Chestnut St. Baptist church, Louisville, the Superintendent of its Sunday-school, and leader of the choir.

Willintina married Charles Bodeker, by whom she has four children, Edwin, Willintina, Fannie and Nellie.

Martha Ellen married Dr. D. B. Miller, but died without issue.

Virginia R. married Dr. D. B. Miller, (her

brother-in-law), and died, leaving two sons, Reuben and Clifford.

Catharine remained single till her death in 1885.

Mary Emily, (the second of the name) died, aged 11 years.

Reuben Broaddus, Sr., the father of the preceding, died in 1865, aged 66 years; Martha, his wife, in 1879, aged 72 years.

Referring back to the children of my grandfather, it may be stated that Edwin, second son of William, learned the shoemaker's trade in Richmond, Va. During his apprenticeship, most of his leisure time was occupied in reading, through favor of a book-seller, who was his friend and gave him access to books. By his fondness for reading, aided by a very retentive memory, his mind became a storehouse of much useful knowledge. He afterwards was chosen Justice of the Peace, in Gloucester county, and held the office many years, being Sheriff of the county four years. He was a Baptist more than fifty years, and for a long time a deacon in a Baptist church. He died in Gloucester county, where he had always lived, except when an apprentice in Richmond, aged 80 years.

Muscoe, oldest son of Edwin, married a Miss Mountcastle, of Richmond. He now lives in Philadelphia, and is an employee of the Baltimore & Ohio Railroad.

William, second son, married Miss Susan Boone, of King and Queen county. He died in 1885.

Virginia, eldest daughter, married W. A. Jones, of New Kent, and resides in King and Queen.

Bettie, second daughter, has never married and resides in Baltimore.

Robert, third son of William, emigrated to Ohio in 1831, married and died, leaving one child, of whom nothing is known.

Warner, fourth son of William, died, aged 19 years.

William, fifth son of William, was a graduate of William and Mary College, and taught school in Middlesex county for a number of years. It is said that his schoolmates all speak in the highest terms of his ability, and that many of the most sensible women of that day were educated by him. Subsequently he engaged in merchandizing, at Churchview, Va., and was so engaged up to the time of his death.

Mordecai, sixth son of William, died in early youth.

Betsy, only daughter of William, married Mr. Robins, of Middlesex, by whom she had several children, of whom four are still living, viz.:

Mrs. Lolla Wright, of Essex, a widow with two daughters.

Broaddus Robins, now with the First National Bank, Richmond, Va.

Albert Robins, a druggist in Richmond, Va.

Mrs. Cell Winston, who, with her husband, lives somewhere in the West.

There are persons of our name in Clarksville, Tenn., Lancaster, Ky., Helena, Ark., and Bloomington, Ind."

Edward Broaddus, (better known as Ned Broaddus), was a respectable farmer. He was killed by two of his slaves, Cato and Patrick. Cato, with an axe, split his master's head open, and then the two, raising a fallen tree, put the body under it to induce the impression that the man had been killed by the fall of the tree. Cato was hung for the crime, and Patrick was transported. "Ned" Broaddus married a Miss Brown, from the southern part of the State, by whom he had one son, Thomas. His wife died soon after the birth of her child. After her death he married a widow Mitchel, her maiden name having been Hickman. By this marriage he had two daughters, Nancy and Sally. I have not been able farther to trace the descendants of "Ned" Broaddus.

Thomas Broaddus, the second son of Thomas (the oldest son of the first settler), was bred a carpenter, but after his marriage engaged in farming, in which he was very successful. He was a man of steady habits, sound sense, and grave and sedate deportment. He died at the advanced age of 83 years. He was twice married. His first wife was Martha Jones, of Essex county, by whom he had three sons, James J., Silas J., and John W., and eight daughters, Sally, Nancy, Elizabeth, Martha, Harriet, Catharine, Emily and Martha Ellen. His second wife was a widow Watkins, by whom he had no children.

James J. Broaddus, oldest son of Thomas, held an honorable position in the community for sobriety and integrity. By industry and good management he accumulated a handsome property and he died at about seventy years of age, respected and esteemed by all who knew him. He was married three times. By his first marriage he had two sons, Albert and William, both of whom died childless; and one daughter, Martha, who married Edmund Sale, and has two sons, Judson, married to Nannie Gouldin, and William, married to Jennie Marshall, and one daughter, Alma, married to James Dillard. By his second marriage, James J. Broaddus had two sons, John, married first to Laura Motley, and afterwards to Lucy Gouldin, and Silas Battaile, who died, leaving seven children by his wife, Sally Gouldin; and two daughters, Emma, who married John Andrews, and died leaving one child, and Sally, married to

Franklin Kidd. By his third marriage James J. Broaddus had no children.

Silas J. Broaddus, second son of Thomas, married a Miss Long, the daughter of a Methodist preacher, and became a very ardent and zealous Methodist. His surviving children are Olin, Wilbur, Irving, Woodford, Sarah and Virginia.

Wilbur Broaddus stands high as a useful citizen and an intelligent and active Christian. Like his father, he is a member of the Methodist Church.

The following is the family record of Thomas Broaddus' daughters :

Sally, married to Goldwin Puller.

Children of this marriage :

Parkinson, John B., James, Ellen, Harriet and Martha.

Elizabeth, married to John Gouldin.

Children of this marriage :

Silas J., Thomas W., Battaile J., George,

James Franklin, Martha J., Lavinia, Virginia, Maria Ann and Betty.

Battaile J., George and Virginia, died unmarried.

Silas J., married Miss Susan Parker. Their living children are John, Silas, Wilton, Louis and Mollie.

Thomas W. Gouldin, married Miss Louisa Redd. Their children are: John, Robley, Wortly, Edmonia, Lucy, Georgie, Nannie, Mollie Lou, Sally and Nelly.

Harriet married Redd Sale.

Their children (both dead) were Thomas R. and Woodford.

Catharine married Robert R. Sale.

The surviving children of this marriage are John O. and Fanny.

Martha Ellen married Andrew S. Broaddus.

Children of this marriage, some of whom are dead:

Oscar, Reuben, Leland, Charles, Clay,

Kingsford, Mary, Betsy, Lucy Ann, Martha Semple, Cornelia, Hattie and Nelly.

A notice of Andrew S. Broaddus' talents and character will be found farther on, when we come to trace the descendants of John Broaddus, the third son of the first Edward.

John Gouldin, who married Elizabeth Broaddus, was a man of unusually strong, though uncultivated intellect. By industry, economy, and wise management, he accumulated a large property. For many years he was a solid, reliable and useful member of a Baptist Church. His son, Dr. Thomas W. Gouldin, was a successful physician, and a most active and influential member of a Baptist Church. He took a leading part in everything that pertained to the interest of his Church, guiding in its discipline, superintending its Sunday-school, leading in its prayer-meeting, and supporting its pastor by his cordial co-operation.

For six years the writer of these lines was his pastor, and, in a pastoral experience of more than forty years, he has known no member of any church with which he has been connected, whom he more highly valued. Dr. Gouldin died in 1884, lamented by his family, and universally regretted by his acquaintances.

The surviving children of John Gouldin are all active and influential Baptists.

Their family record is as follows:

Martha J. married William J. Broaddus. There were no children of this marriage.

Lavinia married William S. White.

Children of this marriage:

George, Jack, William, Andrew, Nannie, Mattie and Callie.

James Franklin, married first, Victoria R. Motley. Children of this marriage: Jack and Burnley. His second wife was Mrs. Virginia Green. Children of this marriage: Robley and Myrtle. His third wife was Miss Virginia Talley. One child, Williamson, is the fruit of this marriage.

Betty, married Lysander B. Conway.

Children of this marriage:

Lizzie, James, Coleman, Powhatan, Lysander B., and Eustace.

Shildrake Broaddus, third son of the first Thomas Broaddus, was a farmer of steady habits and respectable standing. He married Mary Ann Pankey, by whom he had three children: Edwin, Catharine and Mary Ann. It is, I suppose, to this Edwin Broaddus, that W. O. Broaddus refers as "Ned Broaddus," in the following account, furnished by him, of his family descent. He says, "My great grandfather was Ned Broaddus. His wife's maiden name was Polly Pritchet. They moved from Virginia to Kentucky at an early day. They had eleven children, nine sons and two daughters. The sons were Richard,

William, John, Beverly, Jeremiah, Elijah, Whitfield, James and Andrew; the daughters Polly and Betsy. My grandfather, Andrew, came to Missouri and married Grace Askin. He moved back to Kentucky in 1827. He had ten children, seven sons and three daughters: John E., Green B. F., Jeremiah, Andrew W., William F., Sydney C., Elbridge J., Mary, Margaret and Elizabeth. Grandfather, during his stay in Missouri, made one trip to Santa Fe', in company with the famous Kit Carson. While on the trip, my grandfather had the misfortune accidentally to shoot himself through his right hand, and amputation of the arm became necessary. His companions performed the operation with a butcher knife, which, after being used to cut through the flesh, was converted into a saw by hacking the edge, and was then employed in sawing through the bone. The cauterization was done by using a heated king bolt from one of the wagons. [It would seem, from what follows, that this rough surgery did not at all shorten the life of the hardy subject of it.] My grandfather died Dec. 24, 1872; grandmother died Aug. 14, 1876. They left forty-two grand-children and fifty-five great-grand-children. My father, Jeremiah, married Juliet Oldham. There were born unto them eleven children, five boys and six girls: Andrew J., William O., Susan A., Mattie, Elbridge C., Jerry, Gracie, Etta, Eva, Lizzie and Lycurgus."

In the foregoing account, by W. O. Broaddus the very fruitful marriages of his ancestry are worthy of note; though these were by no means exceptional cases in the Broaddus family.

Since the above was written, I have received from Judge Elbridge J. Broaddus, a son of the Andrew Broaddus with the amputated arm, a sketch of his father's family. It is well written, but as it does not differ materially from the sketch furnished by his nephew, Wm. O. Broaddus, I do not copy it in full. It contains, however, some statements not mentioned by Wm. O. Broaddus, that are worthy of record. Elbridge J. Broaddus says of his mother: "The wife of Andrew Broaddus died in July, 1876. It may be worthy of remark that while she was a resident of Missouri, she paid a visit to her friends in Kentucky, and made the trip going and returning on horseback, and thought it nice. She was remarkable for her devotion to her children, and the result of her interest in them for their good, can be seen in the characters of some of them in a marked degree."

Of Green B. Broaddus his brother Elbridge writes: "He was the second son. He died in Kansas. He was First Lieutenant in Humphry Marshall's regiment of mounted rifles in the war with Mexico, and Major of the Seventh

Kentucky Infantry, on the Federal side, in the civil war. He was in several engagements, particularly Perryville and Stone River, at which latter battle he was in command of the regiment. He was repeatedly elected Sheriff of Madison county, Ky."

Elbridge J. Broaddus seems himself to have attained very decided distinction. He was admitted to the bar at Richmond, Ky., in March, 1858. He removed to Chillicothe, Mo., in March, 1867, where he now resides. In 1874, he was elected Circuit Judge of the Seventeenth Judicial District of Missouri, and served six years. He is at present Attorney, in his State, for the Chicago, Milwaukee & St. Paul Railway. His son, Joseph, is a promising civil engineer.

Mordecai Broaddus, fourth son of Thomas, was a successful farmer in Virginia, pursuing that calling all his life. He had a sprightly mind, streaked with a vein of humor, and was a great favorite with his acquaintances. He married Martha Reynolds, by whom he had two sons, Thomas and Mordecai R., and four daughters, Elizabeth, Nancy, Mary, and Fanny. He died aged 71.

Thomas Broaddus, oldest son of Mordecai, by uprightness and benevolence won the respect and esteem of the community, and by sobriety, economy, and good management accumulated a handsome property. He was noted for his kind and cordial hospitality. He died in old age, leaving two sons and two daughters. His oldest son, Dr. C. C. Broaddus, has for many years enjoyed an extensive practice as a physician. His second son, W. W. Broaddus, is a farmer, and is the father of a number of children, with several grandchildren. Thomas Broaddus' daughters are Maria, married to John L. Motley, Rosa, unmarried, and Sarah, the widow of Dr. Alsop. He left a grandson, Richard Campbell, the son of a daughter, Virginia, who died during the life time of her father.

Mordecai R. Broaddus, second son of Mordecai, was a prominent man as a citizen, and as a member of Salem Baptist Church, in Caroline county, Va., of which, for many years, he was a deacon. He died soon after passing middle life. He married Sarah Ann Miller, who died recently in her 76th year, universally esteemed for her many excellent qualities. His surviving children are John P. Broaddus—a man of excellent sense, and unblemished character, and an esteemed deacon of Salem Baptist Church—Thomas, and Attaway, the widow of Captain William Kidd. His oldest son, A. W. Broaddus, died a few years ago, leaving quite a numerous family of children.

John Broaddus, the fifth son of Thomas, was a successful farmer; a man of integrity, industry, and strong sense, but rather stern in his manners and deportment. He married first America Broaddus, daughter of Robin, by whom he had four sons, James H., Mordecai W., John and Warner, and five daughters, Nancy, Mahala, Theresa, Amanda, and Mary. His first wife died at the age of 35. He then married Martha Richerson, by whom he had two sons, Wm. Hyter and Robt. Semple, and one daughter, Jane. His second wife died at the age of 25, and he subsequently married Catharine Gatewood, by whom he had one son, Joseph A., and one daughter, Attaway. He died aged 73. Of the children of John Broaddus, above mentioned, only Amanda (widow of John Gravatt), Mary (widow of —— Puller), Robt. Semple, and Joseph A. survive. James H. Broaddus, the oldest son of John, died leaving two sons, Richard F. and George, and two daughters, Caroline and Agnes. Richard F. Broaddus, oldest son of James H., was a man of sterling worth; sober, industrious, thrifty, upright and religious. After passing, in the Confederate service, unhurt through the four years of the Civil War, he was killed by a fall from his horse a few months after the war closed. He married Miss Virginia Henshaw, by whom he had six children, Maurice E., Willie, Manly, Maxey, Frank, and Effie.

For several years Maurice E. Broaddus has been an acceptable, popular and prominent Baptist preacher. He was educated at the Southern Baptist Theological Seminary. He has held successful pastorates at Camden and at Clinton, S. C., and at present he is pastor of the Baptist Church at Clinton, Missouri. This is a progressive, flourishing, growing church, and the pastor is held in high estimation by the members of his charge, and by the community in which he lives. He is distinguished by a generous nature, cordial and popular manners, and great energy and activity in promoting the cause of Christ in his own field, and by hearty co-operation in all benevolent and religious denominational enterprises. He attends denominational meetings far and near, and is an active and prominent figure at such gatherings. He was a delegate and attended the World's Conference of the Young Men's Christian Association in Berlin, Germany, in 1884. He is in the prime and vigor of robust manhood, married Miss Lillie R. Caldwell, of South Carolina, and has several small children: Mary V., Lucy H., Maurice E. Jr., Edna C., and Robert C. To him the writer is indebted for valuable aid in gathering materials for this history, and publishing the work.

Mordecai W. Broaddus, second son of John, was a prominent and influential citizen, and a popular and useful Baptist preacher. He was especially gifted in hortatory preaching. He died of consumption, in the prime of life, leaving eight children, Joseph B., Robert F.,

William S., John E. (an active Baptist, and an esteemed citizen), Ann Eliza, Virginia, and Betty. Of these only William S., Virginia, John E. and Betty are now living.

John Broaddus, third son of John, lived to be 83 years of age, and died leaving four sons, Mordecai, Christopher, John and Frank, and four daughters, Martha Ellen, Betty, Anna, and Lucy. Warner Broaddus died unmarried. Wm. Hyter died a young man, leaving two children, of whom one, Mary Hyter, wife of O. D. Pitts, survives. Robert Semple lives in Mississippi, and has five children, Aileen, Clemenza, Butler, Robert and Lewelyn. Joseph A. has three children, Ann, Julia and Philip.

John Broaddus' daughters married as follows: Nancy married John Cole, and had a number of children, among them Rev. Robert W. Cole, for many years a popular and useful Baptist preacher. Mahala married Willis Pitts. Her surviving children are Philip,

Oscar, and Mary Susan. Her grandchildren, the children of her son Andrew, who died some years ago, are Geo. Henry, Eugene, Jefferson, Nelly, Lilly, and Nola. Theresa married George Marshall. Only two of her children, James and John, survive her. Amanda married John Gravatt. Her living children are Arthur, Robert, Amanda, Virginia, Sarah, Andrew, William and Ada.

Richard Broaddus, sixth son of Thomas, was for several years a school teacher, and subsequently a farmer. He was also a Baptist preacher of some local note. He married a widow Jeter, by whom he had four daughters, Elizabeth, Nancy, Lucy, and Maria. He died aged 55.

Catharine Broaddus, oldest daughter of Thomas, married Edwin Motley, by whom she had eleven children. Elizabeth, the second daughter, married Goldwin Puller, by whom she had seven children. Ann Broaddus (third daughter) married Captain Robert Sale, and died at 30 years of age, leaving three children.

Of John Broaddus, the oldest son of Edward (the first settler), by his second marriage, Rev. Dr. J. B. Jeter, of Virginia, in a memoir of Rev. Andrew Broaddus, published thirty-five years ago, thus writes: "John Broaddus, son of Edward, was a man of strong and active mind, and well informed; he was first a school teacher, and afterwards a farmer. He was a zealous churchman, bitterly opposed to all dissenters; and his devotion to the Established Church led him to publish one or two pamphlets, intended to confute and ridicule the Methodists, then a young and growing sect. He took part in the fearful struggle which terminated in freeing the American colonies from British domination. He acted as commissary in the army; and on one occasion, expecting the approach of the British troops, he employed his son, Andrew, then a small boy, to conceal his papers in the woods. He married a Miss Pryor, said to be a lineal descendant of Pocahontas, whose blood flows in the veins of so many distinguished families in Virginia. Of this marriage five sons and seven daughters were the bountiful fruit.

William, the oldest son of John, possessed a bright intellect, was liberally educated, and intended by his father for the Episcopal ministry. But alas! how uncertain are all human calculations! He died in his 22nd year, just before the time set for his embarkation to England to receive ordination, changing the cheering hopes of his fond relatives into bitter disappointment and grief. Andrew, though very young at the time of his brother's death, loved him tenderly, and continued to the close of his life to entertain a fragrant remembrance of his virtues, and a lively admiration of his shining talents. He was often heard to say that he thought him not inferior to Pope as a poet. Making due allowance for fraternal partiality, it cannot be questioned that William Broaddus was a young man of rare genius and great merit. His writings and drawings were carefully preserved by his brother Andrew, as an invaluable legacy, until they were, to his deep regret, burned with the house in which he lived."

John Broaddus, second son of the John whose lineage we are now tracing, had unusual mechanical genius. During the Revolutionary war he manufactured many articles for his neighbors, they being cut off from obtaining any thing from England. His first wife was Sarah Zimmerman of Culpeper, by whom he had one child, William. After the death of his first wife he married Mary Ship, of Caroline, by whom he had five children before he left Virginia for Kentucky in 1793. But little is known of him or of his family after he left Virginia.

Of Reuben Broaddus, the third son of John, Dr. Jeter thus speaks, in the memoir before quoted: "Few of the older men, who were accustomed to attend the Dover Association, before its division, can have forgotten the tall and venerable form of Reuben Broaddus. He was a man of sound but uncultivated intellect, remarkable for his prudence, simplicity of manners, and great firmness of purpose—for half a century an efficient deacon of Salem Baptist Church—an arbiter of all neighborhood disputes—a counsellor of the perplexed, and a comforter of the distressed." Reuben Broaddus married Elizabeth Garland, of Gloucester, by whom he had four sons, Christopher, Lunsford, Leland, and Andrew S., and three daughters, Nancy, Lucy, and Eleanor. Of Reuben Broaddus' sons, Christopher and Leland died childless. Lunsford, with quite a numerous family, removed in middle life to Illinois, and but little is known of his descendants. A few years ago two of his sons, Andrew and another whose name is not remembered, came to Virginia on a brief visit. They were evidently men of intelligence and good character.

Andrew S. Broaddus, the youngest son of Reuben, has been prominent as a citizen, a church member and a lawyer. After practicing law several years in Virginia, where he served one session in the Legislature, he removed to Texas in 1854. There he soon secured an extensive and lucrative practice, was for several sessions a member of the Legislature, and for two or three terms a District Judge. He has accumulated a large property, and is a man of influence and high standing in the community in which he lives. He is a man of ardent temperament, of decided character, and of quick and bright intellect. He is a fluent and forcible speaker, an adroit and skilful debater, and a popular and successful advocate. He has been twice

married.   By his second marriage he has no
child; but his descendants, by his first marriage, down to the fourth generation, number
more than a hundred.   Now in his 80th year
he still practices law.

Reuben Broaddus' daughter married ———
Richerson, and died young, leaving one child,
Reuben B. Richerson.   He strikingly re-
sembled his grandfather, Reuben Broaddus,
after whom he was named, both in person
and character.   Like his grandfather, he was
tall .and commanding in stature, and like
him, too, " he was a man of sound, but uncultivated intellect—remarkable for his prudence, simplicity of manners and firmness of
purpose," and like him also, " he was for
half a century an efficient deacon of the
Salem Baptist Church."   Of his children one,
William, was killed at the battle of Antie-
tam; and another, Frank, who was a surgeon
in the Confederate Army, died during the

Civil War. His surviving children are Thomas H., married to Miss Nannie Broaddus, James Reuben, married to Miss Kathleen Butler, and Nannie, married to Dr. Phil. Spindle.

Lucy Broaddus, daughter of Reuben, married Nathaniel Motley. He was an industrious and thrifty farmer, and stood high in the community for integrity and uprightness. The fruit of this marriage was one son, John Leland, and eight daughters, Elizabeth, Christina, Sally Ann, Polly, Laura, Alice, Virginia and Victoria. John Leland Motley is a man of intelligence and integrity, a most respectable citizen, and the Treasurer of Salem Baptist Church, of which his father and grandfather were deacons. He has seven children: Cora, married to Morris Rowe, Laura, John, William, Lilly, Alice and Andrew. Of Lucy Motley's daughters, only Christina, married to W. W. Broaddus, and

Polly, widow of George Marshall, are now living.

Pryor Broaddus, the fourth son of John, had decided mechanical talents, and was mainly occupied in corresponding pursuits. He married Frances Brown, of King and Queen, by whom he had four sons, William, Beverly, Robert and Franklin, and three daughters, Elizabeth, Polly and Emily. He died aged 67.

The youngest son of John Broaddus, whose lineage we are tracing,

REV. ANDREW BROADDUS,

from whom all who have borne his given name have been called, having been the first of the family to become distinguished, and having attained greater eminence than any of them, with one exception, corresponding space, in this history, should be appropriated to a record of his life, and a delineation of

his character. But as he was the father of
the present writer, propriety forbids that such
eulogistic language should be employed by
him in this notice as would be justifiable if
the relationship between the two had been
less close. Happily, however, the author is
relieved of any embarrassment on this point
by being able to substitute, for anything he
might otherwise have been compelled to say,
the language of Rev. Dr. J. B. Jeter, as found
in the memoir of Andrew Broaddus which has
been before mentioned. In quoting from this
memoir, such portions will be omitted as are
considered to be irrelevant to the purposes of
this history, and the omissions thus made,
will not be marked by asterisks; as in this
way, while no injustice will be done Dr. Jeter,
the notice will wear a more connected and
compact form. Dr. Jeter thus speaks:
" Andrew, the youngest son of his father, was
born at the family residence in Caroline

county, Nov. 4, 1770. His childhood gave promise of his future eminence. A thirst for knowledge, and an aptitude to acquire it were among his earliest intellectual developments. He received in all but nine months schooling. Of the manner of that schooling we have no knowledge ; but judging from the systems of instruction then almost universal in Virginia, we may reasonably conclude it was most imperfect. But God had endowed this boy with an uncommon intellect. He early felt in his bosom the kindlings of genius. He thirsted for knowledge as the hunted hart for the water-brook ; and knowledge he resolved to obtain. And what cannot be accomplished by a mind instinct with energy, and firmly resolved ? Andrew educated himself, as, indeed, every really great man, with more or fewer facilities for the work, does. Often, in that day, when the light of candles was a luxury rarely enjoyed by persons in the middle class of society, did this aspiring boy lie flat on his breast upon the floor, poring over his book by the dim light of a pine knot on the hearth. Andrew Broaddus was baptized by his father in the gospel, and his religious guide, Elder Noell, May the 28th, 1789. At his baptism he was united with Upper King and Queen Church, then the only Baptist Church in the vicinity, of which Church he was pastor at the time of his death. Shortly after his baptism, he was called to offer exhortations at the neighboring meetings, and he obeyed the call. His first regular sermon was preached the 24th of December, 1789, at the house of Mrs. Lowrie, in Caroline county. He was ordained to the ministry at Upper King and Queen meeting-house, Oct. 16, 1791, by Theodoric Noell, and R. B. Semple —the first, his spiritual father, and the second destined to be, through a long life, his intimate and devoted friend, his dis-

creet counsellor, and his active fellow-laborer.
Mr. Broaddus commenced preaching the
gospel without a diploma—without a library
—without theological instruction; but he had
what was better than all these—a deep and
experimental sense of the truth, power, and
preciousness of the gospel—a heart glowing
with zeal in the cause of Christ—a mind thirst-
ing for truth, patient in searching for it, quick
in discerning it, and ready in appropriating
and using it, and an elocution natural, graceful, and impressive. Elder Broaddus first
settled in the upper end of Caroline county,
and performed the duties of the pastorate in
Burrus's (now Carmel) Church, and in County
Line. Successively, and for different periods,
the churches called Bethel, Salem, Upper King
and Queen, Beulah, Mangohic (now Hebron),
Upper Zion and others were favored with his
evangelical and instructive ministrations.
Though this was the principal, it was by no

means the only scene of his useful labors. The Baptist Church in Fredericksburg seems to have been gathered and constituted by the joint efforts of Elder Absalom Waller and Elder Andrew Broaddus in 1804. The latter continued to preach there we know not how long after the constitution of the church; but long enough to leave behind him a most pleasing remembrance of his affection, fidelity, and eminent abilities.

In 1821 Mr. Broaddus removed to the city of Richmond, and became assistant pastor, with Rev. John Courtney, in the First Baptist Church. Here he remained—notwithstanding he was greatly beloved, increasingly popular, and had before him an inviting prospect of usefulness—only six months, owing to domestic afflictions, and pecuniary embarrassments. This, so far as we can learn, was his only permanent residence beyond the limits of his native county, and the adjoining county of King and Queen.

But his labors were far from being confined to the churches in which he statedly minister- ed. He was accustomed to make tours, es- pecially in the earlier period of his ministry, into the surrounding counties, everywhere at- tracting large congregations, and by his preaching edifying the godly, and winning the admiration of all.

Few ministers received more flattering offers to settle abroad than did Elder Broaddus. If he remained in his native Caroline it was not because fields wide, pleasing, and full of promise were not opened to him. He was in- vited to accept the pastoral charge, or was corresponded with on the subject of accepting it, by the following churches: The First church, Boston, in 1811 and 1812, to supply the vacancy occasioned by the death of Dr. Stillman; the First Church, Philadelphia, to supply the place of Dr. Staughton; the First Church, Baltimore, in 1819; the New Market Street Church, Philadelphia in 1819; the Sansom Street Church, Philadelphia, in 1824; the First Church, Philadelphia, again in 1825; the Norfolk Church, in 1826; the First Church, city of New York, in 1832; the First Church, Richmond, in 1833, not to mention other calls of minor importance. These invitations to settle in cities and towns, in prominent positions, with wealthy and flourishing churches, paying their pastors generous salaries, he deemed it his duty to decline; partly because he was averse to change, and reluctant to leave his old and tried friends, but mainly because of an unfortunate nervous sensitiveness, which rendered him timid among strangers, and in a great measure disqualified him for laboring in new and exciting circumstances. God marked out for Elder Broaddus the sphere of his activity, and with that sphere he was well content. He was an earnest, diligent, faithful pastor, watching for souls, as one who expected to give account.

He was an eminently studious man. Commencing his ministry with a meagre stock of knowledge, he deeply felt his deficiency, and endeavored, by intense application to study, to supply it. His reading was not extensive, but careful, thorough, and profitable. After a book had passed under his scrutiny its contents were his own, with many emendations and improvements. In most of his books he made, with his pen or pencil, in a neat abbreviated hand, critical notes on the margin. Though not professionally an author he contributed much by his pen to enlarge the views, confirm the faith, and augment the efficiency of the denomination to which he belonged. He early published an octavo volume, entitled, " History of the Bible"—a work highly commended by the leading ministers of different denominations—a work of decided merits, but not much circulated. Many years ago he prepared and issued a Catechism, intended for children, remarkable for its simplicity, and which has lately been re-issued in several editions, and extensively circulated, by the American Baptist Publication Society. At the request of the Dover Association he drew up a form of Church Discipline, scriptural in its principles, and filled with judicious counsels, which was printed and circulated among its churches by that body. A few years since he prepared the Dover Selection of Hymns, which, after a short time, was followed by the Virginia Selection—a large volume containing a greater variety of hymns, and better adapted to the necessities of the churches. Of these, many thousands have been circulated, not only in Virginia, but in other States. Quite a variety of circular letters, written at the request of Associations, essays, addresses, sermons, notes, controversial articles, and letters composed on different occasions, and on subjects of permanent interest, most of which were published either in periodicals or pamphlets, are printed with this memoir.

Elder Broaddus found, amid the varied and pressing engagements of his school, his farm, and his ministry, time for a somewhat extended, though not very frequent correspondence. Among the distinguished worthies, now reposing like himself in the tombs, who enjoyed his confidence and his correspondence, we notice the names of Drs. Baldwin, Allison, Staughton and Mercer, and Elders Leland, Toler, Roper, Absalom Waller, V. M. Mason, Luther Rice, and President Dew, not to name Dr. Semple, his bosom friend, and a host of living worthies. Few of all these correspondents would not readily have subscribed the remark of his early companion and co-laborer, Rev. A. Waller, contained in a letter bearing date March, 1804: "Among the extensive circle of my literary brethren, I am candid to confess that the correspondence of none affords me so much Christian consolation as the letters, which once in a while, I receive from my dear Andrew." The letters of Mr. Broaddus were generally written with great care and taste, and were distinguished for their ease, vivacity and instructiveness.

We are now to contemplate Elder Broaddus in the character of *a polemic*—a character very uncongenial with his meek and quiet spirit. Mr. Alexander Campbell, of Bethany, Va., first made his appearance in Eastern Virginia in the autumn of 1825. His debate on Baptism, with Rev. Mr. McCalla, had then recently been published, and its circulation had prepared the brethren to extend to him a cordial reception. He was considered a learned, able, and fearless defender of the peculiar views of the Baptists; and his own peculiar views, of which little was known, were lost sight of in admiration of his talents. He attended the Dover Association, which in that year was held with the Upper Essex Church, in Essex county, Virginia. Here he was introduced to Semple, Broaddus, Kerr, and the ministers generally of that body. On Lord's day he preached, with Elders Kerr and Bryce. His discourse was long, ingenious, and interesting, containing nothing positively offensive to the fathers in the Association, and remarkable rather for what it denied than for what it affirmed. The sermon was followed by several others of the same general character. His preaching was differently received by different persons; by some it was greatly admired, by some it was disapproved, but the more judicious stood in doubt of it; and all seemed desirous to become better acquainted with his views. This desire enabled him to procure a large subscription list for the *Christian Baptist*, a small monthly pamphlet, which he edited and published in Bethany, and which, after a few years, was merged into the *Millennial Harbinger*—a larger and more respectable periodical. From this time, the *Christian Baptist* became the channel of communication between Mr. Campbell and many persons in Eastern Virginia. This periodical was conducted in a bold, vaunting and bitter spirit; but with considerable ingenuity and force. Gradually, slowly, and cautiously were the peculiar views of Mr. Campbell developed, as the light broke on his own mind, or as he deemed his readers able to receive them. Friendly communications from Semple and others to the *Christian Baptist*, were commented on by the editor with great freedom and severity. These discussions disclosed serious differences between the views entertained by prominent Baptist ministers and the Bethany Reformer.

Elder Broaddus early became a contributor to the columns of the *Christian Baptist*. Never did a polemic possess a more amiable, meek and gentle spirit, or write in a manner more candid, fair and honorable. Melanchthon himself did not excel him in kindness, courtesy, and dignity. Even Mr. Campbell, though accustomed to treat his opponents with little forbearance, was constrained to respect the noble bearing and vigorous talents of his new correspondent. Mr. Broaddus approved what was good, censured what was evil, and attempted to refute what was false in the so-called Reformation. Of all the opponents Mr. Campbell encountered in the early stage of his Reformation, Elder Broaddus was decidedly the most formidable. In him Mr. Campbell met " a foeman worthy of his steel." We hesitate not to express the opinion, that on all important points he gained in the discussion a most decided ad-

vantage over the Reformer. In discrimina-
tion, Biblical knowledge, the power of com-
pressing his thoughts, clearness of style, log-
ical force, courtesy and self-possession, Mr.
Broaddus has had few superiors in the present age.

In 1832 Elder Broaddus was elected to supply the place of the excellent and lamented
Semple, as Moderator of the Dover Association, then the largest Association of Baptist
Churches in the United States, and perhaps
in the world. This office he retained, except
in 1839 when he was absent, till 1841, when
at his own request he was excused from farther
service.

As a man, Elder Broaddus was a noble
specimen. Erect, lithe, of graceful propor-
tions, his person was the finest model of
humanity. A sculptor could not have de-
sired a nobler head for imitation, nor a painter
a finer face for delineation. All his move-

ments were strikingly graceful. Placed
among a thousand men his appearance would
have enlisted the attention, and excited the
curiosity of the spectator. Such was the
casket—a fit depository for a priceless gem.
Mr. Broaddus was unquestionably a genius.
He possessed talents which studies, and professors, and libraries could never have im-
parted to him. He was endowed by nature
with a quick perception, a clear discrimina-
tion, a capacious understanding, an active
imagination, a high appreciation of the beautiful and the grand, and a very retentive memory. He possessed, in no ordinary degree,
the elements of a poet, a painter, and an ora-
tor. We have seen how slender were his
early opportunities for the attainment of an
education; but his genius and application
supplied the place of schools, colleges and
books. He was his own instructor. His literary acquirements, considering his early dis--

advantages, were truly surprising. Few
scholars excelled him in the critical knowledge of the English language. He had some
acquaintance with the Latin, Greek, and
French languages, though his knowledge of
them was not critical. His scientific attainments, though not thorough, were extensive
and highly respectable. His knowledge was
full, ready, and accurate. It is indeed surprising, that, having so little intercourse with
literary society, and no access to large and
select libraries, and possessing comparatively
few books of his own, his information on all
subjects, literary, scientific and theological,
should have been so extensive and thorough.

If such was Andrew Broaddus, reared amid
a comparatively poor, and sparsely-settled
country population, what would he have been
had fortune favored the early and full devel-
opment of his fine genius? We know not.
The mind, as well as the body is sometimes

surfeited. The means of acquiring an education are too frequently converted into the means of indulgence, dissipation and ruin. But our full conviction is, that with the advantages of an early and well-directed education, and a position favorable to the full and vigorous exercise of his mental powers, and a proper improvement of these advantages, and but for his constitutional timidity, he would have been one of the greatest men of this or any other age. But with all his disadvantages, when shall we look on his like again? How rarely do we see a man of intellect so clear, of taste so refined, of knowledge so various, and of eloquence so winning? However brilliant was his genius and ripe his scholarship, it was as a *Christian* that he most brightly shined. He was a man of experimental piety. He not only insisted in his ministry on the necessity of the new birth, but in his life he exemplified the excellence of the change. His piety was sincere, conscientious, habitual and consistent. He was most emphatically a Bible Christian. He studied the Bible with care and diligence, that he might be instructed by its doctrine, directed by its precepts, animated by its examples, comforted by its promises, and inspired with ardor by its prophecies.

The style of Elder Broaddus' sermons was perspicuous, chaste, simple, vigorous and beautiful. His preaching abounded in illustrations. He could find some historical incident, some principle in science, some custom, some object of common observation, to elucidate his theme; and the illustration never failed under his skilful application, to interest and instruct his hearers.

Were we required to describe the power of his oratory by a single term, that term should be *fascination*. There was, in his happy efforts, a most captivating charm. An inci-

dent may best illustrate this remark : more
than twenty years ago, while in the zenith of
his power and popularity, he attended a session of the Baptist General Association held
in the town of L ———. Monday morning he
preached in the Methodist Church to a crowd-
ed audience. Mr. D., a lawyer of distinction
on his way to the Court House, where the
Court was in session, stopped in the street,
beneath the fierce rays of a summer sun, to
listen for a moment to the sermon. Business
urged his departure, but having heard the
commencement of a paragraph, he was intense-
ly anxious to hear its close. Intending every
moment to break away, he became more and
more chained to the spot. Presently he heard
his name called by the Sheriff at the Court
House door, and he soon heard the call
repeated; but it was to no purpose—he was
riveted to the spot. Neither the fatigue of
standing, the melting rays of the sun, the

urgency of business, nor the repeated calls of the officer of the Court could disenchant him. He heard the whole of the sermon, and paid unwittingly the highest compliment to the eloquence of the preacher.

As an author, Mr. Broaddus acquired no mean reputation. His compositions were generally penned with remarkable accuracy and neatness; and his publications were always read with interest and deference. Had he devoted himself to literature, he could not have failed of enviable eminence; but he wrote only at intervals, as he was impelled by the solicitations of his brethren, or by the imperative demands of the great cause in which he was enlisted, and then amid frequent interruptions and the incessant cares of his pastorate. His writings are justly entitled to the praise of perspicuity, ease, elegance and good taste. They abound in weighty counsels, sound expositions of Scripture, convincing arguments employed in a worthy cause, and are imbued with the spirit of piety. They will form an invaluable legacy to the Church, and will be highly appreciated by those who admired and loved him while living. The death of this venerable father was an appropriate termination of a life so pure, so faithful, so useful as his had been. When asked, as his death-struggle approached, what was the state of his mind, "Calmly relying on Christ," was his reply. On another occasion, after he had been silently musing, he characteristically remarked: "The angels are instructing me how to conduct myself in glory." The last words he was heard to whisper were, "Happy! happy! happy!" He fell asleep in Christ on the first day of December, 1848."

To the foregoing sketch of the life and character of the first Andrew Broaddus, extracted from the memoir by Dr. Jeter, I have felt some inclination to append specimens of his composition, both in prose and verse. But I fear that some may think I have already given undue space in this history to the delineation of the character of one man; though that man was the first of the family to become distinguished, though he attained greater eminence than perhaps any of the name, and though that delineation was drawn by a pen other than my own.

I proceed, therefore, to trace the family of this first Andrew Broaddus. He was married four times. His first wife was Miss Fanny Temple, daughter of Col. John Temple, of Caroline. By this marriage he had children as follows: John Wickliffe, who died unmarried; William Temple, who married Fanny Robinson; Eliza S., who married Elliot Chiles; Maria, who married Robert Allen; and Fanny T., who married William Cox.

WM. TEMPLE BROADDUS

and

FANNY ROBINSON, his wife.

Children as follows:

Lucy, widow of Rev. Robert W. Cole.

Mary Eliza, wife of Capt. James Wright.

Edmonia, wife of Mordecai W. Cole.

ELLIOT CHILES

and

ELIZA BROADDUS, his wife.

Children as follows:

Frances, married ——— Johnson.

Sarah, married ——— Duval.

Susan, married ——— Snellings.

Virginia, married ——— Snellings.

Edwin.

Luther.

The last named is a man of superior intelligence, with fine speaking talents, and is a popular and skilful physician.

ROBERT ELLEN

and

MARIA BROADDUS, his wife.

Children as follows:

Robert, Monroe, Andrew, Frances and Lizzie.

WILLIAM COX

and

FANNY T. BROADDUS, his wife.

Children as follows:

Richard H., who married Sarah A. Saunders.

James T., who married Keziah ———.

Richard H. Cox, who died two or three years ago, enjoyed a widely extended and very high reputation as a physician, and was very popular; having represented the county of King and Queen for two or three sessions, in the Virginia Legislature.

James T. Cox was a soldier both in the Mexican War and in the late Civil War. He was killed in the "Capitol Disaster" in Richmond.

Andrew Broaddus' first wife died in 1804 or 1805. His second marriage was with Lucy, daughter of Dr. Robert Honeyman, of Hanover, a gentleman of superior intelligence, of great professional eminence, and of large wealth. By this marriage he had no issue.

After the death of his second wife, Mr. Broaddus was married to her sister, Mrs. Jane C. Broaddus, the widow of Christopher Broaddus. By this marriage he had three children, Wilton H., Andrew and Columbia.

Wilton H. Broaddus, a young man of fine abilities, and of a most amiable disposition, died in 1845.

The second son of Andrew Broaddus, by his third marriage, Andrew, the writer of this record, on the death of his father, in December, 1848, was chosen pastor of two of the Churches—Salem and Upper King and Queen, that had been served by his father up to the time of his death. The pastoral relation then formed has continued uninterrupted up to this time (February, 1888). The writer has occasion for deep gratitude that, during this long period, so many unmerited honors, and such numerous tokens of undeserved respect and esteem have been received by him, not only from the members of the Churches under his charge, but also from a wide circle of friends and acquaintances throughout the State. But he is under special obligations to be grateful for the happy family relations with which he has been favored. These have been due under God, in large measure, to the character of the woman whom it was his good fortune to make his wife nearly fifty years ago. In December, 1838, he married Martha Jane Pitts, and from that time to the present, she has been his loving companion, his wise counselor, and his unfaltering friend. To the support afforded by her constant and tender affection, and to the guidance of her sound

judgment he is indebted, more than to anything else, for any measure of usefulness that
may have marked his life.   Her influence
moulded the character of her children, and
this has been to their parents a source of
gratification and happiness which language is
altogether inadequate to describe.

Of the eight children who were the fruit of
the writer's marriage, only five lived to be
fully grown.   The record is as follows:

ANDREW BROADDUS

and

MARTHA JANE PITTS, his wife.

Their children:

Julian, who married Hallie Terrell.

Luther, who married Eugenie Bryan.

Florence, who married Richard L. Williams.

Andrew, who married Carrie Power.

Mignonette, who is unmarried.

Julian Broaddus, the oldest son, has nine
children, viz: Alfred, Gwin, Florence, Louis,

Andrew, Hallie, Carlyle, Luther and Howard. He is the pastor of the Baptist Church in Berryville, Clarke county, Va. As a preacher, a pastor, a citizen, and a Christian gentleman, he exercises a wide and powerful influence, is respected by all who know him, and greatly beloved by those who know him best.

The second son, Luther, died Oct. 21, 1885, in the prime of life and usefulness, at Newberry, S. C.; where, as pastor of the Baptist Church for nine years, he was honored and beloved as few men have been. He had a vigorous intellect which had been cultivated by close study from his boyhood. He became a "full graduate" of the Southern Baptist Theological Seminary in three years, though beginning without any previous theological reading or any knowledge of Greek. He was a strong, clear, forcible, original, attractive, and eminently Evangelical preacher. His earnest piety, his consecrated and arduous labors, his pure life, his tender sympathy with the suffering and the distressed, endeared him beyond expression to the members of his Church and congregation, while his strong talents and his cordial and gentlemanly manners made him popular with *all* his acquaintances. At the time of his death, he was Vice-President for South Carolina, of the Home Mission Board of the Southern Baptist Convention.

It has rarely happened that the death of a young man has been the occasion of such numerous, tender and loving expressions of mingled sorrow and praise.

Luther left two children, Aileen and Lenore.

Andrew, the third son, has three children, Gay, Carrie and Lois. He is pastor of the Baptist Church at Bowling Green, the county-seat of Caroline county, Va. Though his health is not robust, and though all the members of his family are delicate, yet he labors with great assiduity in his calling. His excellent preaching gifts, his sound judgment, his conservative temper, his amiable disposition, his blameless life, and his cordial manners render him popular, influential and eminently useful.

The oldest daughter, Florence, has one child, Jane Elizabeth, a girl of 16, who is bright, studious and promising. Florence is a woman of enlightened piety, great discretion, superior intelligence, and of engaging and popular manners.

The youngest daughter Mignonette, is unmarried, and lives with her parents; whose comfort and happiness, in their declining years, are greatly enhanced by her thoughtful and tender attentions, her pure character, and her blameless and useful life.

Columbia, the daughter of the first Andrew Broaddus by his third marriage, married Rev. Howard W. Montague, a Baptist minister of strong mind, burning zeal, and great activity and usefulness. He died universally esteemed and respected.

His widow still lives. She is a woman of bright intellect, of engaging manners, of unusual conversational talents, and of enlightened and steady piety. She has two children; Evelyn, who married X. X. Charters, and has one child, Florence, and Andrew P. Montague, who married May Christian, a daughter of Joseph Christian, Ex-Judge of the Supreme Court of Appeals of Virginia. Andrew P. Montague has, for several years, been professor of Latin in Columbian University, at Washington, D. C. He stands high as a teacher, a scholar, a gentleman, and a Christian. Sons of President Garfield, and of Mr. Blaine of Maine have been among his private pupils. He has two small children.

In the Memoir by Dr. Jeter he says of Andrew Broaddus's fourth marriage: "In 1843 Rev.

Mr. Broaddus married Miss Caroline W. Boulware, of Newtown, King and Queen county.
To this lady was granted the honor and privilege of soothing the last years of a life which
had been burdened with its full share of grief
—a service which she performed with exem-
plary delicacy, judgment and affection. She
had only one child, now a little boy three or
four years old, for whose spiritual welfare the
aged parent cherished an anxious solicitude."
Mrs. Caroline W. Broaddus died in 1852, leaving a reputation for gentleness, kindliness,
purity, and earnest and intelligent piety that
has rarely been equalled. William L. Broaddus, the "little boy" mentioned by Dr. Jeter
as the only child of Andrew Broaddus, by his
last marriage, is now a man of over forty
years. He is a Doctor of Medicine, has a
very extensive practice, and enjoys a reputation unequalled, in that part of the State in
which he lives, as a physician of distinguished

skill and success. No man, in all the region
of country around him, wields a more powerful influence for good, or is more highly esteemed for intelligence, integrity, and benevolence. He is a leading deacon in Upper King
and Queen Baptist Church. He married Kate
Macon, the refined and attractive daughter
of the late lamented and beloved Dr. John M.
Garnett, of King and Queen county. He has
nine children—Annie, William, Mary, Kate,
Caroline, John, Reuben, Fanny, and the baby.

One of John Broaddus's daughters—but I
do not know which one—married a man named
Bates. They have only one descendant, a
grandson, William Bates, of Essex county, Va.

Rev. W. A. Gaines, of South Carolina, has
furnished a very full account of the descendants of Susan, or Susannah Broaddus, the
fifth daughter of John Broaddus, and sister of
the first Andrew Broaddus. I give this ac-

count nearly in full, and mostly in Mr. Gaines's language.

EDMUND PENDLETON GAINES

and

SUSANNAH BROADDUS.

Their children :

John	Mary
Robert	Patsey
Silas	Frances
Nathaniel	

Joseph and Benjamin (Twins)

Ezekiel

Two daughters, Mary and Patsey, died in infancy, and Ezekiel died at 16 years of age. Seven of the ten children married. John Gaines, the oldest son, married Kitty Davis, Their record stands thus :

JOHN GAINES

and

KITTY DAVIS.

Their children :

Edmund P	Nancy
William B	Susan
Hayward	Elvira
John	Mary

Robert Gaines' wife's name is unknown.   He raised one son, Edmund P.

SILAS GAINES

and

ELIZABETH ARNOLD.

Their children :

Micajah Berry	Nancy
Henry Johnson	Louisa
	Mary
	Harriet
	Elizabeth

NATHANIEL GAINES

and

CLARISSA ARNOLD.

Their children :

William Arnold	Frances Sarah

Tilman

Rowland

Sandy Walker   Martha Ann

Lawson Presley   Nancy Elizabeth

Marshall Benjamin

Edmund Pendleton

All these sons of Nathaniel Gaines, except the oldest, served in the Confederate Army, two of them, Sandy Walker and Lawson Presley, dying in the service.

FRANCES GAINES

and

ZECHARIAH SMITH.

Their children :

William   Eliza

Ezekiel   Susan

Edmund   Mary

John   Frances

JOSEPH GAINES

and

MISS MORGAN

Had seven children:

Names unknown.

BENJAMIN GAINES

and

NANCY JONES.

Their children:

Joseph   Jane

Susannah Broaddus, wife of Edmund Pendleton Gaines, and progenitor of the Gaineses
who have been mentioned, was probably a
member of a Baptist Church before she left
Virginia, as she united with Turkey Creek
Baptist Church, in Abbeville county, S. C., by
letter.   This church connection placed her
under the pastoral care of Rev. Arthur Williams, one of the soundest, ablest, and most
pious ministers of his time. This privilege
she highly appreciated. She was intelligent,
pious, and greatly enjoyed the public worship
of God, and the company of pious people.
Her fidelity to Jesus was rewarded by tempor-

al and spiritual blessings on herself and her household. She settled the business of the estate, raised her children in comfort, and gave them such education as was afforded by her section of country. Her children all, with possibly one exception, became pious, sooner or later. It is due to facts to spe a k now more at length of her third son, Rev. Nathaniel Gaines. He was in only the twelfth year of his age when his father died. In taste and disposition he was much like his mother, and was from his earliest years strongly inclined to piety. Affectionate, dutiful, fond of home and study, he grew up, not only without any fixed evil habits, but singularly free from any immoral conduct—the pride and hope of his mother.

In those days there were no Sunday Schools. The preaching of Mr. Williams was profound and earnest, but doctrinal rather than persuasive, so that it was hardly expected that children should join the Church. Hence young Gaines, extremely cautious any way, reached the age of twenty-three before he made a public profession of religion. On the 8th day of April, 1821, he was baptized by Rev. Arthur Williams, and was received a member of Turkey Creek Church, of the Saluda Association. From the time of his conversion he had a strong and abiding desire to preach the Gospel. Entering the ministry then was about as slow work as joining the Church. A tedious apprenticeship, under "license to exercise the gift," was about inevitable, and in the absence of better methods for developing the young, was a wise safeguard. His education, while reasonably thorough and accurate, was limited to English, not going beyond the grammar. Anxious to qualify himself for the most efficient service, he wisely resolved to go to Virginia, study in her University, and then spend some time with his maternal uncle, the first Andrew Broaddus, who was then preaching so successfully. But unfortunately the older brothers of the family had married and left the paternal home, and the next younger one had died, so the care of his mother, of the younger children, and of the estate devolved on him. In this dilemma he made the very natural, yet sad mistake—alas! so often made—of sacrificing the future to the present, and remained at home. He, however, persevered in his purpose to preach, and was ordained to the full work of the ministry about the year 1825. From the time he was first licensed he was about fifty-five years in the ministry. He was of vigorous, comprehensive mind, clear, bold, and independent as a thinker, and held the Bible doctrines as expounded by Dr. Gill. He was far ahead of his age in that his reading in public was natural, and his style of speaking conversational. He was of commanding

height, size and figure, with a pleasant voice
and countenance. He enjoyed, in the highest
degree, the confidence and respect of all who
knew him. He inherited some property,
which he increased by judicious management,
and which he wisely used in educating his
children, and starting them in life. In his
81st year a brief and painless illness ended a
life the memory of which is blessed. His
widow, blessed with health of mind and body,
now (Oct. '87) in her 84th year, is living in
pious contentment with her youngest son,
Edmund Pendleton Gaines. One or two incidents will serve to illustrate Mr. Gaines'
character and disposition.

Though naturally of strong will, and of
clear and pronounced convictions, yet he was
a profound lover of peace. When he was of
about middle age a wealthy and kindly young
man married and settled near him. After
a few years a difficulty sprang up between

them, in which the young man was both in fault and was obstinate. A temporary estrangement ensued. Only a few weeks passed, when one morning Mr. Gaines went to the house of the other party, and, after somewhat formal salutations, he said, "Well Mr. J., I have come down this morning just to tell you something that I believe I never told you." "Ah! what is that?" was asked with evident curiosity. Then, with trembling voice and tearful eyes, Mr. Gaines called him by his given name, and said, "I really *love* you." With clasped hands mutual assurances of respect and love followed, sealing, for life, a most cordial friendship.

He was very fond of vocal music, but was opposed to instrumental music in churches. Once he attended church in one of the cities; and, on being asked by his hostess, how he liked the service, he replied: "I enjoyed the budding of Aaron's rod [the sermon] very

much, but didn't like the bleating of his calf"
[the organ].

Mr. Gaines carried out the divine injunction,
"mind not high things, but condescend to men
of low estate," about as conscientiously and
gracefully as was possible for human nature.
In a town where there was considerable wealth
and culture, there lived a pious, but very poor
blind man, having a wife and a large family
of children. Often, when Mr. Gaines would
be in town, instead of riding to church in the
carriage of some one of his many prominent
friends, he would walk a little out of the way,
and escort the old blind man, with his rather
poorly clad family, to church. He would pay
similar attentions to the poorest people anywhere and everywhere that occasion required."

Having traced the descendants of the three
oldest sons of Edward Broaddus (the first

settler), as far as known, we return to follow the line of William, the fourth son. William Broaddus, fourth son of Edward (second son by his second marriage), married Miss Gaines and lived in Culpeper, and is known to have had three sons, William, Thomas, and James. Of these, William was a Major in the America Army during the Revolutionary war. His daughter, Miss Lavinia Deprest Broadus, furnishes the following account of his descendants:

Major William Broadus married first Mrs. Jones. Their daughter, Catharine Wigginton Broadus married Wm. Mills Thomson.

Their children were:

1. Richard Wigginton Thomson, who married Harriet Gardner, of Ohio, by whom he had six children, Mary G., Frederick T., Richard W., Charles, Harry, and Virginia.

2. Mary Juliet Thomson, married Anthony Addison of Missouri. Their children were John

Fayette, Sarah Catharine, Mary Mills, Murray, Olina C., Keturah L., Arthur B., and Anthony Callis.

3. Martha Frances Thomson, married Samuel Campbell. Their children were Martha F., Mary C., Antoinette A., Philip Slaughter, and Robert Francis.

4. William Mills Thomson, married Mary Jane Barker. Their children were Margaret, Catherine, John B., and William Mills.

Juliet Broadus, second daughter of Major William Broadus, married Col. Ward of the United States Service at Harper's Ferry.

Patsy Broadus, third daughter of Major William Broadus and his wife (Mrs. Jones), married Merriwether Thomson, of Harper's Ferry. Their children were William Merriwether, "Jeff." (Confederate General), Betty (Mrs. Abell), Sallie (Mrs. Alfred Duffield), and Emma (Mrs. Dr. Wallace).

Major William Broadus married for his

second wife Martha Richardson, of Richmond, Va. Their children were Sarah Ann and Maria, both of whom are dead, Lavinia, and Mary, who married Thomas Keys, by whom she had six children, two sons, and four daughters. The boys died in childhood, and the surviving daughters reside in St. Joseph, Mo. These daughters are Livy, (Mrs. Moss), Martha (Mrs. Knight, now dead), Annie (Mrs. Dr. Knight), and Mary who is unmarried.

James Broadus, third son of Edward, by his second wife, and brother of William, married another Miss Gaines, sister of the former and half-sister of Judge Edmund Pendleton, and had a son William who was, for many years, Clerk of Culpeper County Court, and familiarly known as "Clerk Billy Broadus" to distinguish him from several other Williams. His son, William Augustus, was long a very popular salesman in stores at Culpeper Court House. He died childless. A daughter married a Mr. Herndon, and her daughter, Nelly, married Mr. Roberts, and left several children.

The following is a condensed record, to be followed by an extended notice, of the descendants of Thomas Broadus, the second son of William:

Thomas Broadus married Mrs. Susannah (Ferguson) White, and had three sons, Edmund, Wm. F., and Andrew, and two daughters, Lucy and Maria.

LINE OF EDMUND BROADUS.

Edmund Broadus, son of Thomas and Susannah Broadus, was born in the county of Culpeper, afterwards Rappahannock, Va., May 5th, 1793.

Nancy Simms, daughter of Edward and Amy Simms, was born September 20th, 1790.

Edmund Broadus and Nancy Simms were

married, at Mountain Garden, in Madison County, February, 1812.

Children of this marriage :

James Madison, born Nov. 30, 1812.

Martha Ann, born July 24, 1814.

Caroline Matilda, born 1822.

John Albert, born Jan. 24, 1827.

Three others, who died in childhood.

Nancy Broadus, wife of Edmund Broadus, died at the University of Virginia, June 22nd, 1847.

Edmund Broadus married Somerville Ward, at Jeffersonton, in the County of Culpeper, 1849.

Edmund Broadus died at the University of Virginia, June 27th, 1850.

Somerville Broadus, widow of Edmund Broadus, died at the home of John A. Broadus, Greenville, S. C., May 28th, 1877.

Descendants of James Madison Broadus :

James Madison Broadus, son of Edmund

and Nancy Broadus, born Nov. 30, 1812. Married Ellen Barbour Gaines, daughter of Capt. Reuben Gaines, Nov. 24th, 1831.

Children of this marriage :

Clarence Linden, born Jan. 24, 1833.

Mary Martha, born Aug. 17, 1834.

Edmund Pendleton, born Sept. 30, 1836.

Ellen B., wife of Jas. M. Broadus, died July 13, 1839.

James M. Broadus and Mary Catharine Lewis were married April 20th, 1843.

Children of this marriage :

Wilmer Somerville, born Feb. 28, 1844.

Thomas Andrew, born Sept. 25, 1846.

Edmund Lamartine, born Aug. 27, 1848.

John James, born Jan. 10, 1850.

Infant son (not named), born May 4, 1851.

Susan, born March 16, 1852.

Rosalie Madison, born Jan. 27, 1855.

Reubenelle Lewis, born Jan. 23, 1857.

William Francis, born Sept. 8, 1860.

John Cooke Green, born Oct. 12, 1862.

Lucy Catharine Moore, born Aug. 8, 1866.

MARRIAGES.

Clarence L. Broadus, son of James M. and Ellen B. Broadus, married Sarah Kemp.

Children of this marriage:

Thomas Madison, born May 8, 1856.

Ellen Barbour, born Sept. 6, 1858.

Mary M. Broadus, daughter of James M. and Ellen B. Broadus, married Dr. George H. Leitch, about 1859.

Thomas A. Broadus, son of James M. and Ellen B. Broadus, married Sallie J. Botts, Sept. 15, 1873. They have one child, Edmund Kemper, born Aug. 26, 1876.

DEATHS.

Edmund Pendleton Broadus, son of James M. and Ellen B. Broadus, died Nov. 8, 1838

Edmund Lamartine, son of James M. and Mary C. Broadus, died April 10, 1849.

Infant son, died June 14, 1857.

Susan, died December, 1852.

Wilmer Somerville, died Aug. 27, 1856.

John James, died August, 1857.

William Francis, died ——, 1863.

Lucy Catharine Moore, died Aug. 9, 1866.

James M. Broadus, father of the above named children, and son of Edmund and Nancy Broadus, died at his home, in Alexandria, Va., July 21st, 1880, aged sixty-seven years.

Mary M. Leitch, daughter of James M. and Ellen B. Broadus, and widow of Dr. George H. Leitch, died Feb. 28th, 1881.

Family record of Martha Ann Broadus and her descendants:

Martha Ann Broadus, daughter of Edmund and Nancy Broadus, born July 24th, 1814. Married Edmund Bickers, July 24th, 1845.

Died, June 6, 1874.

Children of the above marriage:

Anne Carter Bickers, born Aug. 9, 1846.

Sarah Martha, died at 18 months of age.

John Edmund, died at $3\frac{1}{2}$ years of age.

Carrie Willie, born Aug. 10, 1852, died Aug. 29, 1870.

Anne Carter Bickers, daughter of Edmund and Martha Ann Bickers, married John Micou Farrar, Sept. 17th, 1865.

Children of this marriage :

William Edmund, born Aug. 13, 1866.

James Madison Broadus Bickers, born Feb. 20, 1873, died Oct. 5, 1874.

Thos. Leitch, born Mar. 25, 1875.

John Albert, born Mar. 12, 1877, died Nov. 7, 1880.

Martha Lee, born Jan. 13, 187:).

Howard Micou, born May 15, 1885.

Mercer Garnett, born April 21, 1887; died soon after.

Caroline Matilda Broadus, daughter of Edmund and Nancy Broadus, married Rev.

Wm. A. Whitescarver Jan. 18th, 1849, and died, childless, Aug. 25th, 1852.

John Albert Broadus, (now known as Dr. John A. Broadus), the youngest child of Edmund and Nancy Broadus, gives an account in a sketch which will presently appear, of his own immediate family, and some others who have not heretofore been mentioned; I pass therefore to

THE LINE OF WILLIAM F. BROADDUS.

William F. Broaddus, son of Thomas and Susannah Broadus, born April 30th, 1881, died Sept. 1876.

Married Mary Ann Farrow, Oct. 28th, 1819.

Children of this marriage :

Edmund Samuel Broaddus, born Nov. 22, 1820.

Amanda F., born July 23, 1823.

Wm. Henry Crawford, born June 13, 1825.

Mary Louisa, born June 17, 1827.

Thomas E., born May 17, 1830.

John F., born Mar. 15, 1838.

Mary Ann Broaddus, wife of Wm. F. Broaddus, died Sept. 8th, 1850.

Wm. F. Broaddus married Mrs. Susan Burbridge in Kentucky, July 29th, 1851. She died childless, April 21st, 1852.

Wm. F. Broaddus married Mrs. Lucy Ann Fleet in Virginia, April 21st, 1853. The only child of this marriage, Lucy Maria Broaddus, was born Feb. 17th, 1854.

Marriages of Wm. F. Broaddus' children:

Edmund Samuel married Sarah Jane Rust, of Warren County, Va.

Amanda F. married John Keen, of Loudoun County, Feb. 14, 1840.

Mary Louisa married Francis Webb, of Kentucky, Nov. 11, 1845.

Wm. H. Crawford married Ann Dudley, of Kentucky, in 1846.

Thomas E. Broaddus married Kate Gaines Mahan, of Kentucky, in 1858.

Sarah Jane, wife of Edmund Samuel Broaddus, died March 25, 1841, and in 1846 he married Bettie A. Baker, of Lexington, Ky.

DEATHS.

W. H. C. Broaddus, son of Wm. F. and Mary Ann Broaddus, died Aug. 9, 1850.

Amanda (Broaddus) Keen, died in 1860.

Louisa (Broaddus) Webb, died ——————

Lucy Maria Broaddus, died Nov. 8, 1861.

John F. Broaddus, died Feb. 4, 1887.

Wm. F. Broaddus, father of the above, died Sept. 1876.

Lucy Ann Broaddus, 3rd wife of Wm. F. Broaddus, died Dec. 1881.

Grandchildren of Wm. F. Broaddus :

John Fauntleroy Broaddus, son of E. Samuel and Sarah J. Broaddus, born Feb. 10, 1841.

Children of E. Samuel and Bettie A. Broaddus :

F. Webb, born Dec. 14, 1847.

Mary Elizabeth, born Mar. 26, 1849.

Wm. Amos, born May 24, 1850.

Willie Crawford, born Dec. 31, 1846.

Edmund Samuel, born Dec. 31, 1851.

Thomas Parker, born Mar. 6, 1854.

Willie Crawford Broaddus, son of W. H. C. and Ann Broaddus, was born Sept. 22, 1847.

Children of Francis and Mary Louisa (Broaddus) Webb:

Crawford Broaddus, born Sept. 20, 1846.

Mary Farrow, born June 13, 1848.

Lucy Woodward, born April 11, 1850.

Nannie Susan, born Feb. 29, 1852.

Frank, Jr., born Jan. 7, 1854.

Kate Todhunter, born April 3, 1855.

Mosely Hopkins, born Dec. 16, 1856.

Charlton, born Dec. 23, 1857.

Bessie May, born Aug. 27, 1859.

Children of John and Amanda (Broaddus), Keen :

Mary E., born Jan. 21, 1841.

George Broaddus, born Oct. 19, 1842.

Crawfordella, born Nov. 20, 1846.

Martha Louisa, born Feb. 5, 1844.

John Samuel, born May 15, 1848.

Nannie Blanche

John Willie

Thomas

Charles Fox

Child of Thomas E. Broaddus and Kate Gaines Mahan:

Paul Broaddus.

DEATHS.

Crawfordella Keen, Aug. 4th, 1848.

Martha Louisa Keen

George Broaddus Keen

Mary (Keen) Plaster

John Samuel Keen, Aug. 1880.

John Willie Keen, 1886.

Frank Webb, Jr., June 16, 1854.

Kate Todhunter Webb, Mar. 9, 1856.

Charlton Webb, Oct. 11, 1863.

LINE OF ANDREW BROADDUS, THIRD SON OF THOMAS.

Andrew Broaddus, born in 1809; died March 4th, 1868. Married Dec. 31st, 1828, to Mrs. Belle Simms, widow of Dr. John Simms, to whom she had been married, at the time of his death, only six weeks.

Children of this marriage :

Mary Susan, born Sept. 1833.

Virginia, born June, 1835.

Andrew, born Dec. 11th, 1840.

Lucy P., born Mar. 31, 1851.

Louisa W., born April 12, 1853 ; and six children who died in infancy.

Andrew Broaddus, son of the Andrew who married Mrs. Belle Simms, was married Sept. 5, 1865, to Miss Bettie C. Lionberger of Luray, Va.

Children of this marriage:

John A. Broaddus, aged 20 years.

Lillie B. Broaddus, aged 18 years.

Eugenie Broaddus, aged 15 years.

Bessie Broaddus, aged 13 years.

Lucy Broaddus, aged 12 years.

Two children have died, Mary Constance, who died in infancy, and Edmund who died at the age of five. Mary Susan Broaddus, daughter of Andrew and Belle Broaddus, married first Maxy Sangster, an influential citizen and merchant, of Covington, Indiana. He died in 1863. Her second husband is J. L. Loveland, Mayor of Clyde, Cloud County, Kansas. By her first marriage she had three children, a son, and two daughters. Both daughters have died. The son, Thomas E. Sangster, lives in Kansas. There have been no children by the second marriage.

Virginia Broaddus, daughter of Andrew and Belle, married Thomas M. Almond, of Luray, now a prominent merchant of Lynchburg, Va. Virginia died in 1870, a bright Christian.

Louisa W., another daughter, married John W. Rosson, a merchant of Culpeper County, Va. They have one child, a son.

The following is the sketch, by Dr. John A. Broadus, of which it was said, a few pages back, that it would presently appear:

The three brothers, William, Thomas, and James (sons of William), probably after their father's death, began to spell their name Broadus. There is a tradition that they were led to do so by a somewhat eccentric maternal uncle, who was fond of objecting to the use of unnecessary letters in words. There are many similar cases of slight divergence in the spelling of family names, as Brown, Browne, Broun; Thomson, Thompson; and probably Leigh and Lee. Thomas Broadus, who died in 1811, expressed a wish that his sons should return to spelling the name Broaddus, and William F. and Andrew, who were children at the time, did so. But Edmund, being already a teacher, with some business relations, feared business complications if he should make the change. Descendants of Edmund and those of Major William Broadus, are probably the only persons who now spell the name with one *d*; also some who have Broadus as a middle or first name.

Edmund Broadus was named after Judge Edmund Pendleton, a Judge of the Supreme Court of Appeals of Virginia, and a half brother of his grandmother. His father lived among the spurs of the Blue Ridge, in the upper end of what was then Culpeper, and is now Rappahannock county. Edmund taught school in the family of Edward Sims, (afterwards spelled Simms), a farmer of some means, and gave the entire proceeds for the first year to his mother, to meet some debts left at the death of his father. Marrying Miss Nancy Simms, daughter of Edward, he continued several years in that neighborhood, teaching school and keeping a mill, and afterwards moved down the country to within a few miles of Culpeper Court House. Nearly every male descendant of Thomas Broadus, and of his brother James, has spent part of his life as a school-teacher. After some years Edmund became a farmer and a Militia Major, and at length began to represent Culpeper county in the House of Delegates, which he continued for twenty years, with one or two voluntary interruptions, but without ever being beaten in an election. He quit the support of President Jackson upon the famous "Removal of the Deposits," and was always afterwards a Henry Clay Whig. It has frequently been declared by former associates in the Legislature, that he was, for some years, leader of the Whig party in the House of Delegates. At one time, a caucus of the party, when in the majority, offered to elect him Governor; but he declined, on the ground that the Governor's expenses beyond the salary would consume all his property. He was from youth an earnest Christian, and early became an active church member, and in the course of years the most influential member of the Shiloh Baptist Association. When the Temperance movement began, he early took an interest in it, and after some years announced to his friends that if a candidate for re-election to the House of Delegates, he would utterly abandon the then universal practice of "treating." Amid abounding ridicule, wrath, entreaties and doleful predictions, he led an active canvass and was elected.

He was often called on as a peace-maker, to settle difficulties between individuals, or strife in churches. He was not a highly eloquent man, being deficient in imagination and the swell of passion; but he was strong in argument, clear in statement, well acquainted with his subjects and with human nature, happy in quiet humor, and able to carry the sympathies of those who heard him. Going as a member of a Legislative Committee to investigate certain riots at the University of Virginia, he was strongly urged by his old friend Joseph C. Cabell, then Rector of the University, to take charge of a new "State department" designed to give free tuition and cheapened board to one student from every senatorial district. He removed to the University in 1846, chiefly because it would give his youngest son the opportunity of becoming a student, and died there in 1850.*

James Madison Broadus, son of Edmund, spent his early life in Culpeper as teacher and farmer. He became connected with the Virginia Midland Railroad when first built, and was for twenty years General Ticket Agent for the road, up to his death. As deacon of the Baptist Church in Alexandria, the hospitality of his home became famous. He

---

* With the exception of the immediate family of John Albert, the names of the descendants of Edmund Broadus, with dates of births, marriages, and deaths, have already been given; hence they are omitted here (except when given incidentally in the description of character) though given in the original of the above sketch. A. B.

was a man of remarkable gifts, seeming to be in all respects born for public speaking; but in childhood he contracted, by imitation of a servant, an impediment in his speech, which grew excessive, and through life made it impossible to carry out his manifest calling.

John Albert Broadus, youngest child of Edmund, was educated chiefly by his father and his sister Martha, and afterwards at the famous boarding-school of his maternal uncle, Albert G. Simms, in Culpeper. After teaching three or four years, he entered the University of Virginia in 1846, and was graduated Master of Arts in 1850. He was married Nov. 13, 1850, to Maria Carter Harrison,* who died Oct. 21, 1857. The children of this marriage were Eliza Somerville, born Oct. 1, 1851; Annie Harrison, born Sept. 17, 1853, married May 17, 1878, to Rev. Wickliffe Y. Abraham, (their son John Broadus Abraham,

* The daughter of Dr. Gessner Harrison, of the University of Virginia. A. B.

born Aug. 30, 1880); and Maria Louisa, who died in childhood.

While teaching one year in the family of Gen. John H. Cocke, on James River, in Fluvanna he preached frequently, having begun to preach in 1849, and been ordained in 1850. From 1851 to 1853, he was assistant instructor of Latin and Greek in the University, and at the same time pastor of the Charlottesville Baptist Church. The latter position he held till 1859, but from 1855 to 1857, was temporarily released from duty to be chaplain to the University, the assistant pastor of the Church being Rev. A. E. Dickinson, now of the *Religious Herald.* In 1859, Mr. Broadus became Professor in the Southern Baptist Theological Seminary, then established at Greenville, S. C., which was his home till in 1877 the Seminary was removed to Louisville, Ky. In 1863 to 1865, the Seminary was suspended in consequence of the war. He preached some months of 1863 as a missionary in Gen. Lee's army; but finding that his health would not bear this, he became Corresponding Secretary to a Sunday school Board of the Southern Baptist Convention, then established at Greenville to supply the destitute schools. The Board published, on Confederate paper, about one hundred thousand primers, question books, hymn books, etc., and distributed them throughout the accessible States, together with twenty-five thousand Testaments, sent through the line by the American Bible Society. Mr. Broadus was married a second time, Jan. 4, 1859, to Charlotte Eleanor Sinclair, of Albemarle county, Va. Besides two children of this marriage who died early, there are the following five:

Samuel Sinclair, born Jan. 10, 1860.

Caroline, born Feb. 21, 1863.

Alice Virginia, born Feb. 10, 1867.

Ella Thomas, born April 19, 1872.

Boyce, born Nov. 24, 1874.

William F. Broaddus, son of Thomas, became a preacher while quite young. He early broke away from the influence of certain "Old School" or "Hardshell" Baptist ministers, and for a number of years was in Northern Virginia the recognized leader of the "Missionary Baptists." He was a pastor of four country churches, and at the same time a busy school teacher. It was his favorite theory that a preacher ought to be also a teacher, and he adhered to this during most of his life. He was a preacher of great popular power, skilful in argument, clear in statement and exposition, overwhelming in passionate exhortation, and overflowing with kindly humor, which sometimes appeared even in his sermons, and in private brightened every circle. He long maintained a famous boarding school for both sexes at Middleburg, Loudoun county, Virginia. Though declining invitations to pastorates in Baltimore, Philadelphia, and elsewhere, he removed, about 1840, to Lexington, Ky. Having spent some years as pastor in that place, he went to Shelbyville, Ky., and again established a boarding school, always preaching to surrounding churches. After the death of his second wife he returned in 1852 to Virginia. During most of his remaining years he was pastor at Fredericksburg, where he had a female school : but when driven out of that town by military operations he became pastor at Charlottesville, Va., and remained there several years after the war, then returning to Fredericksburg, where he died. During the years immediately following the war he traveled much to collect funds for the support of soldiers' orphans in different parts of the State, arranging by correspondence through friends to have them attend neighboring schools, and paying the tuition from his collections; public schools not having then been established. Dr. Broaddus was a man of very rich natural endowments and extremely versatile; but his native facility, and his persuasion as to the propriety of teaching, prevented his maintaining in later life the habit of close study. He was a singularly wise and kindly pastor, and showed the same traits in the prominent part he always took in the work of the Baptist General Association of Virginia. With all his marvellous humor and wit, his inexhaustible fund of attractive anecdote and his brilliant repartee, he seemed never to use these powers in a way to give others pain; and he appeared sincerely to enjoy a joke at his own expense, even more than at the expense of others.

Andrew Broaddus, third son of Thomas, after preaching a short time in the vicinity of Luray, Va., labored as a Baptist preacher for a number of years in Northeastern Missouri, and afterwards for several years in Kentucky.

chiefly as Corresponding Secretary of the Baptist General Association. At the outbreak of the war he entered what was finally called Gen. Lee's army, as a missionary, and continued to the end of the war, laboring with extraordinary zeal and usefulness, especially in the way of holding protracted meetings in camps where there was no chaplain. His principal work after the war was as agent in Missouri for the Southern Baptist Theological Seminary.

He was a man of clear intelligence and deep insight into human nature. He was overwhelmingly earnest, and as often happens, he coupled with this a highly humorous turn, which expressed itself, sometimes even in the pulpit, in a very quaint and curious fashion. His unselfishness, and thorough consecration to the work of the ministry, were manifest to all.

Andrew Broaddus, son of the last-mentioned,

graduated at Georgetown College, Ky., and was a Lieutenant in Gen. Lee's body guard of cavalry. Since the war he has lived at Luray, having been a member of the State Legislature, and being now clerk of two courts, and editor of a local newspaper, and said to be the most popular man in the county. He is a zealous Baptist, markedly hospitable, and always ready to do any one a kindness—a man of superior intelligence and admirable character.

Lucy Broadus, daughter of Thomas Broadus, and sister of Edmund, Wm. F. and Andrew, married her maternal cousin William Ferguson, and they early removed to Illinois, where she died in 1871, and her husband in 1872. Of about twelve children it is said that three or four are now living, including one son.

Maria Broadus, sister of the above Lucy, was born about 1805, and married John Strother Wallis. She died in 1831, in Virginia, and her husband in 1839, in Illinois.

They had four children, besides one who died in childhood. Sarah Wallis married Mr. Stafford, of Illinois. Her two sons, Albert Russell and Willie, and her daughter, now Mrs. Mary Boyce, all live in that State. Thomas Oliver Wallis was a popular youth in Winchester, Va., where he died at the age of nineteen. Mildred Wallis married Mr. Saunders, of Rappahannock Co., Va., and died about 1880. Mary Russell Wallis, the youngest child, has long lived at Lexington, Ky.

James Broadus, son of William Broaddus, and brother of Major William and of Thomas, was an ensign in the Revolutionary Army, and afterwards a militia Major. He was born Dec. 27th, 1756, and married Miss Ann Ferguson, sister to the wife of his brother Thomas. Their children were Elizabeth, born Sept. 15, 1782, and died in Virginia, unmarried, in 1862; Catharine (or Katy) Gaines, born Jan. 26,

1787; William D., born May 16, 1789, married when advanced in life, and died about 1850, in Culpeper county, without offspring ; Sarah, born July 8, 1792; Edward Watkins, born Dec. 15, 1795, died in 1810; James Gaines, born Aug. 3, 1800; Susan Coleman, born Dec. 9, 1803.

Of the above, Katy Broadus married Thomas N. Butts. After living some time in Fredericksburg, and in Albemarle and Culpeper counties, Va., they removed to Missouri, where Mr. Butts died in 1862, and the wife in 1884.

Their children are as follows: Ann Elizabeth, born November, 1806, married Preston Lawrence in 1826, and died Aug. 12, 1881. Ellen N., born February, 1809, married Nathaniel Hinkle, of Western Virginia, in 1839, and died in Utica, Mo., 1884. James M., born April, 1811, married Elizabeth Yager, of Madison county, Va., in 1832, and the wife died in 1852. William M., born November, 1813, married, in 1843, Jane Yager, who has died, but the date is not ascertained. Martha F., born Feb. 4, 1816, married, in 1839, to Washington Brannel of Western Virginia. Juliet A., born Oct. 27, 1818, married in 1842 to John S. Harper, of Albemarle county, Va., died in Utica, Missouri, Dec. 28, 1884. Thomas E., born April, 1821, married in 1851 to Martha Johnson, of Franklin Co., Mo., and died in 1874. Sarah C., born Feb. 12, 1826, married in 1844 to Charles Harper, of Albemarle county, Va. All the children of the family except the last three were baptized in Culpeper county by "old Father Garnett."

Sarah Broadus, daughter of the above James, married James Burdett, of Rappahannock county, Va. Their children were James Broadus, Susan and Crawford. James Broadus Burdett in 1871 married Mary Morton Woods, of Charlottesville, and lives at Culpeper Court House. Their children are James Morton and Gertrude Lee.

James Gaines Broadus, son of the above James, was married Feb. 1824, to Elizabeth Susan Gaines, daughter of Capt. Reuben Gaines, of Culpeper. The wife died in 1863, and the husband in 1865. Their children were Lucy Ann, Ellen Catharine, Elizabeth Frances, James Henry, Susan James, Sally Judson, and four younger ones who died in infancy. They have all lived for the most part in Culpeper County, Va. Miss Lucy Ann died at Culpeper Court House, in 1886, after a life of highly intelligent and earnest Christian usefulness. Miss Ellen Catharine died soon after she was grown; and so did the son James Henry. Elizabeth F. was married, December, 1847, to Bernard G. Gordon, and died in 1848. Susan James was married Oct. 21, 1858, to Rev. Richard H. Stone. They spent some years in the Yoruba country, Central Africa, as missionaries; but were compelled to return on account of the wife's health, and have ever since lived at Culpeper Court House, where Mr. Stone is principal of the public schools, and preaches to Baptist churches in the surrounding country. Their children, besides one who died in infancy, are Lucy Broadus, Richard Taylor, James Henry, Mary Conway, Ellen Barbour, and John.

Sally Judson Broadus, daughter of James G., was married in Oct. 1867, to Bruce William Stringfellow, of Culpeper county. Their children are Ann (who died in 1876), Richard, Susan Blanche, James Broadus, Lucy Ann, Robert, Eliza, Bruce William and Sally Richard Elna Moore ("Dixie.")

James G. Broadus was a teacher, land surveyor, farmer and a Baptist deacon. He was a man of penetrating intelligence, sound judgment, massive character and earnest piety, who commanded the profound respect of all who knew him.

Susan Coleman Broadus, daughter of James, and sister of James G., was married June 17, 1839, to Frederick Burdett, brother of the above mentioned James Burdett, but residing in what is now the State of West Virginia, where she died July 12, 1866. The grandson of Mr. F. Burdett's former marriage is the well known humorous writer, Robert Burdette, who maintains the family tradition by being a Baptist deacon. The children of Susan Coleman Burdett, are Sarah Amanda, born Aug. 5, 1840; Columbia Frances, born July 2, 1842; Martha Catherine, born Nov. 13, 1843; Selina Susan, born 1845, died 1850. Of these, Sarah Amanda was married in 1862, to John V. Martin, who died in 1876. Their children, besides two who died in infancy, are Frederick Thornton, Marian Kate, Jessie Burrus, Elizabeth Broadus, Bernard Leslie and

Arthur George. Columbia Frances Burdett was married in 1868 to Andrew J. Stone; their children, besides two who died in infancy, are Mary Ferguson, Mattie Burdette, Lizzie Hamilton, Florence Belle, Ida Blaine.

I add some notes about other branches of the family than my own. I requested Rev. W. A. Gaines, of Gaines, S. C., to write you a full account.* I knew his father, Nathaniel Gaines, a Baptist preacher in Abbeville county, S. C., who told me that his grandmother was the sister of Andrew Broaddus. He was a good man, having the confidence of all, and showed extraordinary familiarity with the text of the English Bible. His son, William A. Gaines, is a man of decided intelligence and excellent character, and has been the useful pastor of various Churches in South Carolina. Another son, Rev. Tilman R. Gaines, after some years in the pastorate, has

---

*See notice of the Gaines family in a preceding part of this volume.
                                              A. B.

devoted himself to various enterprises of publication and immigration. A daughter of Nathaniel Gaines married Mr. Ramsey, of Greenville county, S. C., and their son, Rev. David G. Ramsey, is a graduate of Richmond College, and of the Southern Baptist Theological Seminary, and now pastor in Tuscaloosa, Ala.

I add the following, obtained from Mrs. Robert McAllister, of Kentucky. Richard Broaddus came from Virginia to Madison county, Ky., and married Miss Bohon. His children were Rev. George W. Broaddus, who lived and died in Madison county, a Baptist preacher; Hudson Broaddus, who removed to Missouri; Wilson, who died in Madison county; and a daughter who became Mrs. Estell, and lives in Missouri. Hon. D. R. Francis, Mayor of St. Louis, is a relative of theirs. Rev. George W. Broaddus married Miss Hunt, relative of George Hunt, D. D.

Of their children, Kate is Mrs. Robert McAllister, living near Stamford, Ky.; John, who studied at Georgetown College, lives near Georgetown, having married Sally Rochester Ford, a niece of Rev. S. H. Ford, D. D.; George W., a graduate of Center College, Ky., is engaged in teaching.

To the foregoing sketch of the members of his branch of the Broaddus family, written by Dr. John A. Broadus, it is proper I should add my own estimate of some of the persons therein mentioned, and especially of the writer of the sketch himself.

Major Edmund Broadus, the oldest son of Thomas, deserved all, and much more than all that is said of him in the preceding sketch. His conservative temper, sound judgment, strong intellect, unswerving integrity and spotless life commanded the admiration and won the confidence of his acquaintances, while the influence of his deep religious character was felt by all who knew him. His life furnished striking proof that it is possible— however difficult it may be, to unite with decided political opinions, and active partici- pation in political life, unblemished integrity and shining Christian graces. For thirty years an ardent politician, and for twenty years a political office-holder, yet through all this period he continued to grow in grace and knowledge, and in influence and activity as a Christian. Happy would it be for our country if such men as he generally filled the offices, State and Federal. Had he accepted the place of Governor of Virginia, urged upon him by his party, he would have been a worthy successor of the illustrious men who had previously filled the Executive chair of the State.

Few men have been so widely respected and esteemed while they lived, and so gener- ally lamented when they died as was James

Madison Broadus. His intelligence and integrity, and his consistent and active Christian life commanded the respect and esteem of his acquaintances, while his cordial yet dignified manners, and his abounding and hearty hospitality won the warm regard of his many friends. But for an unfortunate impediment of speech, acquired in childhood and growing with growing years, he would have been a man of marked distinction.

No one who has borne the Broaddus name, or shared the Broaddus blood, attained such eminence as

REV. JOHN A. BROADUS, D. D., LL. D.,

the youngest son of Major Edmund Broadus. In the sketch he has furnished for this volume he simply says that "he entered the University of Virginia in 1846, and was graduated Master of Arts in 1850." Of course he does not say, what it is proper, however, I should

John Albert Broadus.

add, that he graduated with the highest honors of the Institution, and that among the distinguished alumni of that famous school none
have reflected greater lustre on their *Alma
Mater* than he. The bare facts of Dr.
Broadus' life will be found in the sketch he
has written, and hence they are omitted here.
I confine myself to a tribute—a very imperfect
and inadequate one it will prove—to his
talents and character. For profound and
varied learning, and for distinguished talents
as a preacher, a teacher, and a writer he has
not only a national, but also a European reputation. He is one of the most fascinating of
preachers. His charming simplicity of style,
his winning manner, his chastened and cultivated fervor, his clear conception of the truth
and his capacity to make it clear to others,
and his apt and striking illustrations capti-
vate and carry away his audience whenever
he preaches. His love of learning, his

patience, his talent for lucid explanation, and his deep interest in his pupils render him one of the most successful, and, at the same time, one of the most popular of teachers. As a writer he enjoys a wide and well deserved reputation.

In addition to articles of decided merit in Magazines and Reviews, and extensive writing in the *Religious Herald* and other newspapers, he is author of several books that are destined to live long after he is dead. His two books, on the Preparation and Delivery of Sermons, and on the History of Preaching, are accepted as standards on the subject of which they treat, and much used as text-books in Theological Seminaries. His volume of Sermons and Addresses has, within a very short time, reached a second edition, and he has lately completed, after twenty years toil, a Commentary on the Gospel of Matthew (published by the American Baptist Publication Society) which, for varied and profound scholarship, accurate analysis, clear exposition, eminently evangelical sentiment, striking illustrations, and deep and reverential piety, is without a rival. In the nature of the case, Dr. Broadus' reputation is necessarily more *extensive* as a preacher and a writer, than as a teacher. Yet persons, who have the capacity, and have had the opportunity to form a correct judgment, regard him as an unequalled teacher. His work as a teacher has been distinguished by a self-denial and devotion as rare as its fruit has been bounti ful and blessed.

In 1859, Drs. James P. Boyce, John A. Broadus, William Williams and Basil Manly, became the first professors in a Theological school, at Greenville, S. C., called the Southern Baptist Theological Seminary. The school was endorsed by the Southern Baptist Convention, who had a right to nominate its trustees, and who have always given its interests a place in the programme of their annual meetings. The undertaking, however, did not at first meet universal favor among the Baptists of the South. Some were opposed to Theological schools; regarding them as human factories for turning out men-made preachers. Others, who favored Theological education, yet feared that the iron-clad curriculum, then ruling in nearly or quite all Theological schools, would be adopted in this one, and that thus the freedom and force which had distinguished Southern Baptist preachers would be sacrificed to precision and formality. The Seminary has conquered this opposition, and has proved these fears to be groundless. The course of instruction is so flexible, that men of every measure of capacity, and widely differing in preparation may secure its benefits, while, at the same time, it is so extensive and thorough, that the highest attainments in linguistic and Theological learning may be reached by those who have the capacity to acquire them, and the time and inclination to seek them. When the Civil War broke out, the Seminary was in its infancy, just struggling to its feet. It owned no property, its endowment was subscribed, but not collected, and its library and other school appliances were meagre. The exercises of the Seminary were necessarily suspended during the war; and at its close, the prospects of the Institution, like those of almost every Southern College, seemed utterly hopeless. The people, overwhelmed by misfortune, stripped of their property, sad and disheartened, seemed ready to sink under their burdens, into despair. The struggle for bread appeared to demand every thought and effort. To attempt the maintenance of an unendowed Theological school among a people thus stripped and peeled, appeared to many to be folly. And it would have been folly, but for the dauntless courage, the arduous toils, and the consecrated self-denial of John A. Broadus, James P. Boyce, and their associates. Offers of desirable pastorates, which had frequently been previously made to Dr. Broadus, became about this time, more numerous and urgent than ever. He was earnestly solicited to take charge of large, wealthy and intelligent city Churches— North and South, paying munificent salaries. He was also invited to be Professor or President in numerous Colleges and Universities throughout the country. Though Dr. Broadus was by no means insensible of the advantages and enjoyments afforded by such positions, yet he resolutely turned away from them, and gave himself to the arduous toils, the wearying anxiety and the stern self-denial incident to building up the Seminary from the ground among a poverty-stricken people.

And now he has his reward. The Seminary is established on a firm basis. It owns a splendid lot in Louisville, Ky., on which a noble building is just completed. It has an endowment of $250,000, with a prospect that this amount will soon receive material and needed increase, and more than 150 young men are receiving instruction at the hands of its professors, making it one of the largest Theological schools in the world. The fruit borne by the Seminary, during the twenty-three years that have elapsed since the close of the war, is believed to be unequalled in the history of similar institutions. During this period hundreds of young men have come out from the Seminary, admirably equipped mentally and spiritually for their life-work. In our own country, and in foreign lands, they have been instrumental in converting thousands, and in founding and building up uncounted Churches. And all this has been due, in large measure, to the example, the counsels, and the instructions of Dr. Broadus and his associate Professors. Dr. Broadus is about sixty years old, and is in the prime of intellectual vigor, while, by his prudence and temperance, he has so strengthened a naturally delicate physical constitution that there is good ground to hope for him yet many years of usefulness and honor.

REV. WILLIAM F. BROADDUS, D. D.,

was the second son of Thomas and Susannah Broadus. His family record, and the prominent incidents in his life have been previously recorded in this volume. His only surviving child, Dr. Thomas E. Broaddus, of St. Louis, Mo., is reported to me as an accomplished gentleman, and a prominent and successful physician.

Dr. Wm. F. Broaddus' opportunities for education were only such as were furnished by

Rev. Wm. F. Broaddus.

neighborhood schools; bnt he had a vigorous intellect and an ardent temperament, and was distinguished by tireless industry and unconquerable energy, and, like many men who have made their mark on the generation in which they lived, he, in large measure, educated himself. Such were his attainments and reputation that when he reached middle life, Columbian College, at Washington, conferred on him the title of Doctor of Divinity. To Dr. Broaddus more than to any other man are the Baptists of Northwestern Piedmont, Virginia, and of the valley of the Shenandoah indebted for their present prominence, influence, and numbers. He commenced preaching in the county of Culpeper when quite young, being scarcely more, I believe, than twenty years of age. When he entered the ministry there were, in all the region round about, very few Baptists except such as were known as "Hard Shell" or "Black Rock" Baptists. These were quite numerous. Some of them were persons of intelligence and of respectable social position, but most of them were uneducated, and were as narrow and bigoted as they were ignorant. They were violently opposed to missions, Sunday Schools, and all religious associations and enterprises that seek the conversion of men and the promotion of the cause of Christ. Some of them were antinomians, and all of them were predestinarians of such a pronounced type that they regarded it as presumption in a preacher to appeal to sinners to repent, and folly in sinners to seek repentance till impelled to it against their will by a supernatural and resistless Divine inpulse. Their ministers were uneducated, but some of them were men of vigorous intellect, and they denounced with great fervor, at great length, and in violent, and sometimes abusive language the " New Lights" as they called those who dared to urge men, by exhorting them to repent, "to take the work of God into their own hands." Among these people Wm. F. Broaddus appeared, and excited no little commotion. Young, ardent, of pleasing manners and fine personal appearance, with a bright intellect and attractive speaking gifts, he soon won the attention and admiration of the people, while, at the same time, he drew upon himself the fiercest assaults of the " Hard Shell" preachers. But he was equal to the occasion. His imperturbable good humor, his keen wit, his facility of speech, his insight into human nature, and his adroit management gave him the advantage in every contest, and constantly strengthened his influence. He was a tireless laborer. Riding on horseback over the rough mountains, living on the coarse fare and sleeping in the rude huts of the mountaineers, he was, day in and day out, employed in preaching in groves, in log cabins, in private houses—anywhere

and everywhere that a congregation could be
gathered.   Making the tail of a wagon, a
stump, or a rock his pulpit he poured out the
truth from a burning heart, and carried the
people with him.   Soon a reaction commenced
and it has gone on till all that region, once
dead through Black Rockism, is now alive
with active, earnest, progressive Baptists.

Probably the most conspicuous feature of
Dr. Broaddus' mental constitution was his
taste and talent for the humorous. Of this
trait numerous illustrations were furnished in
his intercourse, during a long life, with all
sorts of people.   One case may be mentioned
as a sample, though the effect of Dr. Broaddus'
humor, as is true of humor generally, de-
pended, in large measure, on voice and manner.   During the Civil War the city of Fredericksburg was sometimes held by the Confederate, and sometimes by the Federal
troops.   At one time when the latter had pos-

session, a number of the prominent citizens of the place—among them Dr. Broaddus—were arrested, on some charge or suspicion not now remembered, and carried prisoners to Washington. On reaching Washington the prisoners were brought for examination before an officer; when the following colloquy took place between him and Dr. Broaddus:

Officer—" What is your name?"

Dr. B.—"William F. Broaddus."

Officer—" What does F. stand for in your name?"

Dr. B.—"I don't know."

Officer—(Angrily). " Now sir, I will not put up with evasions or impertinence. Tell me at once what F. stands for in your name?"

Dr. B.—I don't know. My mother named me William Francis Ferguson Broaddus. When I grew up to be a youth of some size I thought it looked awkward to have two F's in the middle of my name, and I asked my mother's permission to drop one. To this she consented ; but I have never known whether I dropped the F. that stood for Francis, or the F. that stood for Ferguson."

Officer—"Where were you born ? "

Dr. B.—"In Virginia."

Officer—" In what county ? "

Dr. B.—"I don't know."

Officer—(Exasperated) "I want none of your foolishness. Answer the question ex-plicitly and at once."

Dr. B.—"I was born in what at the time was the county of Culpeper; but since that time the county of Rappahannock has been formed from Culpeper and the place at which I was born was cut off with Rappahannock county. Now if I should say I was born in Culpeper that would not be true, because the place at which I was born is not in Culpeper. If I should say I was born in Rappahannock that would not be true, because there was no such county when I was born. I wish you would tell me in what county I *was* born." By this time the officer began to appreciate the humor of his prisoner, and pressed him with no farther questions ; and when he was released (which was within a few days) he left the prison with the regrets and kindly regard of all connected with it.

It is greatly to be regretted that an auto-biography, written and re-written by Dr. Broaddus, and to which reference is made in the extracts given below, was lost. Doubtless that autobiography contained not only inter-esting incidents in Dr. Broaddus' life, but also a valuable record of facts and occurrences of a general character. From a mere fragment, left by Dr. Broaddus at his death, the follow-ing extracts are given :

"In very early life I had formed a habit of recording in such a diary as an observant boy of 10 or 12 years might be expected to write

the passing incidents of my boy-days. Later
in life, but before I was of mature age, I re-
wrote this diary, putting it in better form,
and adding to it such incidents as memory
supplied, so that at about 20 years of age I
had a pretty well connected sketch of such incidents of my youthful life as seemed to me
worth recording. This practice I continued
till I was about 50 years old, when my dwell-
ing, a large Female Academy, was burned [at
Shelbyville, Ky.] and all the diary, number-
ing then about seven pretty large manuscript
volumes, written in very small hand, was
utterly destroyed. This was a severe loss to
me. Having then been for thirty years a minister of the Gospel, I had kept a register of
the sermons I had preached, the names of the
persons I had baptized into Christ, the names
of the parties whom I had married, with many
notes and memoranda of facts and incidents,
such as were deemed appropriate in noting

the progress of a man's life who had devoted
his time and talents from an early period
jointly to the work of the Gospel Ministry
and to the instruction of youth. Unwilling
that my whole life should be utterly forgotten, I resumed my Diary in 1850, and, at the
same time, began to re-write, as best I could
from memory, some of the more prominent incidents of my past life. This I continued, at
intervals, up to the year 1862, by which time
I had re-written the past record, that had been
burned, as far as the year 1845, and had kept
up the Diary from 1850 to 1862. But in
November 1862 the town of Fredericksburg,
where I then resided, was bombarded by the
United States forces, and the town sacked and
plundered, and my entire records of my past
life either carried away or destroyed. And
now (January 1872) utterly discouraged as to
any prospect of accomplishing what I had
fondly hoped would greatly interest some

whom I shall leave behind me, I had given up
all further expectation of leaving behind me
any written record.

But recently being confined at home by
inclement weather in mid-winter, and also by
infirm health, I conclude, once more, to write
a sketch of my life—or rather *commence* it.
How much of it I may finish no man can
know."

Though the whole of the fragmentary auto-
biography, from which the above extract is
made, is interesting, yet the only other portion
of it, which seems suited to these pages, relates
to the name of the church with which, on their
baptism, his mother and Dr. Broaddus united,
and which is given by him as follows:

"This Church received its name in the following singular manner. At an early day,
when the county of Culpeper, Va., was a mere
wilderness, and persons could travel only in
by-paths and on horseback, a certain spring,

near the place now called F. T., became quite famous, for travellers stopping and refreshing themselves with water and such food as they could carry with them. On a certain occasion one Francis Thornton, of King George county, Va., was travelling with a company of friends, through this region. They stopped at the aforesaid spring which broke out under the shade of a large beech tree. Mr. Thornton cut the initials of his name (F. T.) on this beech tree. In a short time travellers through this region would direct strangers to the F. T. spring—calling it by his initials. After the county became somewhat settled a blacksmith's shop was put up near the spring, and called the F. T. blacksmith shop. Still later a country tavern was established called the F. T. tavern; and when, at last, the Baptists erected a church house in this region it was called the F. T. Church."

REV. ANDREW BROADDUS, OF KENTUCKY,

the youngest son of Thomas and Susannah Broaddus, though born, reared, married, and living for several years in Virginia, and afterwards for many years in Missouri, yet returning toward the close of his life, from Kentucky, where he had also resided several years, to Virginia, was called, in his later years (in order to distinguish him from others of the same name), "Andrew Broaddus of Kentucky." He was a man whose high character and admirable qualities commanded the respect of all who knew him, and won the love of all his connections and friends. He was cheerful, yet never frivolous—amiable and gentle yet firm and decided. He was a zealous, untiring, consecrated, intelligent, acceptable and successful Baptist preacher. It was the privilege of the writer to have him preach at his church, during the late war, and to spend several days in his company. His hopefulness, amiability, deep and earnest piety, and persuasive and evangelical preaching made an impression on all who heard and saw him that will never be effaced. A statement, made to me at that time, furnishes a striking illustration of his hopefulness, piety and cheerful acquiescence in the dispensations of Providence. He said that he had just written, by the underground railroad, to his daughter who was across the line in what was then regarded as the enemy's country. He had written to his daughter that he hoped and believed the Confederacy would be successful; but that if it should turn out otherwise, and he should be made Mr. Lincoln's boot-black, and his wife Mrs. Lincoln's washer-woman, he should still sing,

"Children of the Heavenly King,
As ye journey sweetly sing."

His widow, Mrs. Belle Broaddus, resides

with her only son, Andrew, at Luray, in Page county, Va. She is justly esteemed a mother in Israel. She is noted for her remarkable cheerfulness, her affectionate disposition, her sympathetic benevolence, and her active and intelligent piety. Her son, Andrew Broaddus, of Luray, is, in the best sense of the term, a gentleman, refined, intelligent, courteous, and manly. His delightful home, secured by his own thrift and indomitable energy, is the abode of a bounteous and cordial hospitality, and is adorned not only by the presence of his venerated mother, but also by that of his intelligent and attractive sister, Lucy, his sweet wife, and his interesting children.

Having traced the lineage of the Broaddus family as far as the information in my possession enables me to go, I close this history with some general remarks suggested by the facts that have been mentioned. While it is not known to the writer that any Broaddus lives in a New England or Middle State, persons wearing the Broaddus name may be found in all the Southern States, in nearly, or quite all the Southwestern States, and in many of the Western and Northwestern States. In addition to these there are hundreds, known by other names, whose lineage may be traced, on the one side or the other, to a Broaddus. The descendants of the first pair who emigrated from Wales and settled on Gwyn's Island doubtless numbered several thousand. One of them, R. W. Thompson, of Indiana, whose mother was a Broadus, was a member of Mr. Hayes' Cabinet. With this exception no member of the family is known to have occupied high official position, and but two may be regarded as having become decidedly eminent in other walks of life. Several, however, have been distinguished, and not a few have been prominent and influential. They have belonged, generally, to the middle class of respect-

able people, and have been marked by aver-
age intelligence and education, while some of
them have been persons of superior intellectual gifts, and of much more than ordinary attainments. Few of them have been professional men. There have been among them
some merchants, quite a large number of
teachers, a few physicians, and a few lawyers,
several of them distinguished. They have
lived very largely in the country, engaged in
the peaceable pursuits of agriculture—a few of
them being mechanics.

There have been a few unworthy characters
among them; but the overwhelming majority
have been persons of upright lives, and of un-
impeachable standing. It is not known that
any person of that name was ever arraigned
before a court of Justice, charged with a crime
or a misdemeanor. The Broadduses have generally—almost universally—made a profession
of religion in early life; and nearly all of them

have united with the Baptists; the only exceptions being found among those who have become connected, by marriage, with persons belonging to some other denomination. The family has been unusually fruitful in preachers, the writer having been personally acquainted with twelve Baptist ministers belonging to it. Both as ministers and laymen the Broadduses have been active, prominent and effective in seeking to subdue the world to Christ. To their personal efforts and influence in this direction they have added the hearty support of all the educational and missionary enterprises controlled by the denomination to which they have belonged. They may justly claim to have had no insignificant share in securing tne prominence and progress reached by the Baptists of the South and West within the past half century.

He that "setteth the solitary in families" has been especially favorable and gracious to

the family of which the writer is a member,
and he desires, in closing this Family History,
to acknowledge, with humble gratitude, his
indebtedness for mercies peculiarly rich and
unmerited, even when compared with those
bestowed on his favored kindred.

———

After this volume went into the hands of the printer a
full sketch of the descendants of Edward Broaddus was received from his grandson, W. J. Broaddus, of Erwin, Tenn.
I very much regret that it did not come to hand in time
to be inserted in the book.   There is, however, a sketch of
the descendants of Andrew Broaddus, a son of Edward, by
his grandson W. O. Broaddus.   A. B.

DESCENDANTS OF

EDWARD BROADDUS,

THE

PROGENITOR OF THE BROADDUS FAMILY

IN AMERICA.

FIRST GENERATION.

EDWARD BROADDUS WHO CAME FROM WALES.

SECOND GENERATION.

First wife of EDWARD BROADDUS unknown.

Children— 1 Thomas.

2 Richard.

3 Dolly.

Married MARY SHIPP. (2nd wife.)

Children— 4 John.

5 William.

6 James.

7 Shipley.

8 Robin.

9 Elizabeth.

177

THIRD GENERATION.

1

THOMAS BROADDUS married Miss ANN REDD.

Children— 10 Edward.
11 Thomas.
12 Shildrake.
13 Mordicai.
14 John.
15 Richard.
16 Redd.
17 Catharine.
18 Elizabeth.
19 Ann.
20 Sarah.

2

RICHARD BROADDUS married Miss —— ——

Children— 21 Edward Broaddus.

3

DOLLY BROADDUS.

Descendants not known.

4

JOHN BROADDUS married Miss FRANCES PRYOR.

Children— 22 William.
23 John.
24 Reuben.
25 Pryor.
26 Andrew.
27 Lucy.
28 Mary.
29 Frances.
30 Elizabeth.
31 Susannah.
32 Martha.
33 Hannah.

5

WILLIAM BROADDUS married Miss GAINES.

Children— 34 William.
35 Thomas.
36 James.

6

JAMES BROADDUS married Miss GAINES.

Children— 37 William.

7

SHIPLEY BROADDUS married Miss CONNALLY.

Descendants unknown.

8

ROBIN BROADDUS married Miss SARAH HARWOOD.

Children— 38 Warner.
39 William.
40 Robert.
41 Mary.
42 Caroline.
43 America.

9

ELIZABETH BROADDUS married RICHARD GAINES.

Children— 44 Pendleton.
45 James.
46 Polly.
47 Elizabeth.

FOURTH GENERATION.

10

EDWARD BROADDUS married Miss BROWN. (1st wife.)

Children 48 Thomas.

Married a Miss MITCHEL. (2nd wife.)

Children— 49 Nancy.
50 Sally.

11

THOMAS BROADDUS married Miss JAMES. (1st wife.)

Children— 51 James J.
           52 Silas J.
           53 John W.
           54 Sally.
           55 Nancy.
           56 Elizabeth.
           57 Martha.
           58 Harriett.
           59 Catharine.
           60 Emily.
           61 Martha E.

Married a Miss WATKINS. (2nd wife.)

No Children.

12

SHILDRAKE BROADDUS married Miss MARY A. PANKEY.

Children— 62 Edwin.
           63 Catharine.
           64 Mary A.

13

MORDECAI BROADDUS married Miss MAY REYNOLDS.

Children— 65 Thomas.
           66 Mordecai.
           67 Elizabeth.
           68 Nancy.
           69 Mary.
           70 Fanny.

14

JOHN BROADDUS married Miss AMERICA BROADDUS. (1st wife)

Children— 71 James H.
           72 Mordecai W.
           73 John.
           74 Warner.
           75 Nancy.
           76 Mahala.
           77 Theresa.
           78 Amanda.
           79 Mary.

Married Miss MARTHA RICHERSON. (2nd wife.)

Children— 80 William H.
81 Robert S.
82 Jane.

Married Miss CATHARINE GATEWOOD. (3rd wife.)

Children— 83 Joseph A.
84 Attaway

15

RICHARD BROADDUS married Mrs. JETER.

Children— 85 Elizabeth.
86 Nancy.
87 Lucy.
88 Maria.

16

REDD BROADDUS.

17

CATHARINE BROADDUS married EDWIN MOTLEY.

Children— 89 William.
90 John.
91 Richard.
92 Elizabeth.
Six others, names unknown.

18

ELIZABETH BROADDUS married GOLDEN PULLER.

Children— Seven, names unknown.

19

ANN BROADDUS married ROBERT SALE.

Children— Three, names unknown.

20

SARAH BROADDUS.

21

EDWARD BROADDUS.

Emigrated to Kentucky in 1801.   Wife's name unknown.

Children— 94 James.
             95 Richard.
             96 Elizabeth.
             97 Whitfield.
             98 Beverly,
             99 Elijah.
             100 John.
             101 Thomas.
             102 Jerry.
             103 William.
             104 Polly.
             105 Andrew.

23

JOHN BROADDUS married Miss SARAH ZIMMERMAN.

Children—106 William.

Married Miss NANCY SHIPP. (2nd wife.)

Children—107 Daughter. (name unknown) and four
              others

24

REUBIN BROADDUS married Miss ELIZABETH GARLAND.

Children—108 Christopher.
             109 Lunsford.
             110 Leland.
             111 Andrew S.
             112 Mary.
             113 Lucy.
             114 Eleanor.

25

PRYOR BRODDUS married Miss FRANCES BROWN.

Children—115 William.
             116 Beverly.
             117 Robert.
             118 Franklin.
             119 Elizabeth.
             120 Emily.

26

ANDREW BROADDUS married Miss FANNIE TEMPLE.

Children—122 Wickliffe.
        123 William T.
        124 Maria.
        125 Eliza.
        126 Fannie T.

Married Miss HONEYMAN. (2nd wife.)
    No children.

Married Mrs. JANE BROADDUS. (3rd wife.)

Children -127 Wilton H.
        128 Andrew.
        129 Columbia.

Married CAROLINE BOULWARE. (4th wife.)

Children—   William Lee.

31

SUSANNAH BROADDUS, married EDMUND P. GAINES.

Children—130 John.
        132 Robert.
        133 Silas.
        134 Nathaniel.
        135 Mary.
        136 Patsy.
        137 Frances.
        138 Joseph.
        139 Benjamin.
        140 Ezekiel.

34

WILLIAM BROADDUS married Miss JONES.

Children—141 Catharine.
        142 Wigginton.
        143 Juliet.
        144 Patsy.
        145 Richerson.

Married MARTHA ———. (2nd wife.)

Children—145 Sarah A.
        146 Maria.
        147 Lavinia.
        148 Mary.

35

THOMAS BROADDUS married SUSANNAH WHITE.
Children—149 Edmund.
150 William F.
151 Andrew.
152 Lucy.
153 Maria.

36

JAMES BROADDUS married MARY A. FURGUSON.
Children—154 Elizabeth.
155 Catharine.
156 William D.
157 Sarah.
158 Edward W.
159 James G.
160 Susan C.

37

WILLIAM BROADDUS married Miss ——.
Children—161 William A.
162 Daughter, name unknown.

39

WILLIAM BROADDUS married ELIZABETH MOTLEY.
Children—164 Reuben.
165 Edwin.
166 Robert.
167 Warner.
168 William.
169 Mordecai.
170 Betsy.

43

AMERICA BROADDUS married JOHN BROADDUS.
Children given before 71-79.

FIFTH GENERATION.

51

JAMES J. BROADDUS married Miss ——.

Children—171 Albert.
172 William.
173 Martha.
174 John.
175 Silas B.
176 Emma.
177 Sally.

52

SILAS J. BROADDUS married Miss LONG.

Children— Olin.
Wilbur.
Irving.
Woodford.
Sarah.

54

SALLY BROADDUS married GOLDEN PULLER.

Children— Parkinson.
John B.
James.
Ellen.
Harriet.
Martha.

56

ELIZABETH BROADDUS married JOHN GOULDIN.

Children—178 Silas J.
179 Thomas W.
180 Battaile J.
181 George.
182 James F.
183 Martha J.
184 Lavinia.
185 Virginia.
186 Maria A.
187 Betty.

58

HARRIET BROADDUS married REDD SALE.

Children—   Thomas R.
             Woodford.

59

CATHRINE BROADDUS married ROBERT R. SALE.

Children—   John O.
             Fannie.

61

MARTHA E. BROADDUS married ANDREW S. BROADDUS.

Children—   Oscar.
             Reuben.
             Leland.
             Charles.
             Clay.
             Kingsford.
             Mary.
             Betsy.
             Lucy A.
             Martha S.
             Cornelia.
             Hattie.
             Nellie.

62

EDWIN BROADDUS married POLLY PRICHETT.

Children—188 Richard.
         189 William.
         190 John.
         191 Beverly.
         192 Jeremiah.
         193 Elijah.
         194 Whitfield.
         195 James.
         196 Andrew.
         197 Polly.
         198 Betsy.

65

THOMAS BROADDUS married Miss ——.

Children—199 Cornelius C.
200 William Woodson.
201 Maria.
202 Rosa A.
203 Sarah.

66

MORDECAI BROADDUS married SARAH A. MILLER.

Children— Woodford.
Preston.
John P.
Thomas.
Attaway.
Susan.

71

JAMES H. BROADDUS married Miss GATEWOOD.

Children—204 Richard F.

Miss BOULWARE. (2nd wife.)

Children— George.
Caroline.
Agnes.

72

MORDECAI W. BROADDUS married Miss ——.

Children— Joseph D.
Robert F.
William S.
John E.
Annie F.
Virginia.
Betty.

73

JOHN BROADDUS married Miss ——.

Children—
Reuben.
Mordecai.
Christopher.
John.
Frank.
Martha E.
Betty.
Ann.
Lucy.

75

NANCY BROADDUS married JOHN COLE.

Children—
Robert W.
William.
R. Mordecai.
Daughter.

76

MAHALA BROADDUS married WILLIS PITTS.

Children—
Philip.
Oscar.
Mary S.
Andrew.

77

THERESA BROADDUS married GEORGE MARSHALL.

Children—
George W.
James.
John.
Eliza.

78

AMANDA BROADDUS married JOHN GRAVATT.

Children—
Andrew.
William.
Robert.
Arthur.
Amanda.
Virginia.
Sarah.
Ada.

80

WILLIAM HYTER BRAODDUS married Miss ——.

Children—   Mary.

81

ROBERT S. BROADDUS married Miss MILLER.

Children—   Eugene.
Helen.
Aileen.
Clemenza.
Butler.
Robert.
Llewellyn.
Sally.

83

JOSEPH A. BROADDUS married MARY GATEWOOD.

Children—   Ann.
Julia.
Philip.

94

JAMES BROADDUS married Miss ——.

Children—   Martha married Mr. Kidd.
Nancy married Mr. Patterson.
Jane married Mr. Roland.
Mildred.
Betsy.
Susan.
Jane.
William.

95

RICHARD BROADDUS married MARY NEWLAND.

Children—   Hudson married Miss Reid.
Sally married Daniel Surgeon.
Wilson married Miss Cruse.
205 Geo W.
206 Beverly.
Edward Nicholas.
—— married Nancy Ballard.

96

ELIZABETH BROADDUS married JOHN JARMON

Children—   Polly married Mr. Epperson.
              Sally married Mr. Price.
              Edward.
              Waller.
              Beverly.

97

WHITFIELD BROADDUS married Mrs. BALLARD.

Children—207 Elijah.
              Nicholas Edmund.

98

BEVERLY BROADDUS married Mrs. FRANCES REDMOND.

Children—   Edward.
              Benjamin F.
              William.
              Mary J.

99

ELIJAH BROADDUS married MARY BARNETT.

Children—208 Joseph E.
         209 Martha A.

100 .

JOHN BROADDUS married MARY BROADDUS.

Children—   Franklin.
              Mary E.
              Martha.

Married Mrs. WALKER, (2nd wife.)
Children—   Eliza.
              Julia.
              John.

101

THOMAS BROADDUS married Miss NEWLAND.

Children—   Amelia.
              Martha.
              Mary.

102

JERRY BROADDUS married Miss ——.

Children— Mary.
Margaret.
Missouri.

103

WILLIAM BROADDUS married JANE E. MOORE.

Children— James.
Thomas.
Henry C.
210 William J.
211 Richard S.
212 Margaret J.
213 Mary I.

104

POLLY BROADDUS married THOMAS FRANCIS.

Children— Susan married Mr. Ballard.
Mary married Mr. Ballard.
Jane.
Elizabeth.
Thomas.
William.
Louis.
Edward E.

105

ANDREW BROADDUS married Miss ——.

Children— Edward.
John.
Andrew.
James.
Francis.
William E.
Richard.
Mary.
Margaret.

106

Miss BROADDUS daughter of John Broaddus married a
Mr. BATES.

Children— William Bates, Essex Co., Virginia.

109

LUNSFORD BROADDUS married Miss ——.

Children—   Andrew. Several others.

111

ANDREW S. BROADDUS married MARTHA E. BROADDUS.

Children—   See Martha E. Broaddus 61.

113

LUCY BROADDUS married NATHANIEL MOTLEY.

Children—214 John Leland.
                Elizabeth.
            215 Christina.
                Sally A.
            216 Polly.
            217 Laura.
                Alice.
                Victoria.
                Virginia.

114

ELEANOR BROADDUS married Mr. RICHARDSON.

Children—218 Reuben B.

115–121

Children of Pryor Broaddus the writer has no account of.

123

WILLIAM T. BROADDUS married Miss FANNY ROBINSON.

Children—219 Lucy.
            220 Mary E.
            221 Edmonia.

124

MARIA BROADDUS married ROBERT ALLEN.

Children—   Robert.
                Monroe.
                Andrew.
                Francis.
                Lizzie.

125

ELIZA BROADDUS **married** ELLIOTT CHILES.

Children—222 Frances.
223 Sarah.
224 Susan.
225 Virginia.
Edwin.
Luther.

126

FANNIE T. BROADDUS **married** WILLIAM COX.

Children—226 Richard H.
James T.

128

ANDREW BROADDUS **married** MARTHA J. PITTS.

Children—227 Julian.
228 Luther.
229 Florence.
230 Andrew.
Mignonette.

129

COLUMBIA BROADDUS **married** Rev. H. W. MONTAGUE.

Children—231 Evelyn.
232 Andrew.

130

WILLIAM LEE BROADDUS **married** KATE M. GARNETT.

Children— Annie.
William.
Mary.
Kate.
Caroline.
John.
Reuben.
Fannie.
Robie.

131–140

GAINES Family.

142

WIGGINTON BROADDUS **married** WILLIAM MILLS THOMPSON.

Children—233 Richard W.
         234 Mary Juliet.
         235 Martha F.
         236 William Mills.

143

JULIET BROADDUS **married** COLONEL WARD.

144

PATTY BROADDUS **married** MERRIWETHER THOMPSON.

Children— William M.
          Jeff.
     237 Bettie.
     238 Sallie.
     239 Emma.

145–148

Children of Martha Richerson.

149

EDMUND BROADUS **married** S. NANCY SIMMS.

Children—240 Jas. Madison.
     241 Martha A.
     242 Caroline M.
     243 John Albert.

150

WILLIAM F. BROADDUS **married** MARY A. FARROW.

Children—244 Edmund S.
     245 Amanda F.
     246 Wm. H. C.
     247 Mary L.
     248 Thomas E.
     John F.

Married Mrs. LUCY E. FLEET. (3rd wife).

Children— Lucy Maria.

151

ANDREW BROADDUS married Mrs. BELLE SIMMS.

Children—249 Mary Susan.
       250 Virginia.
           Andrew.
           Lucy P. .
       251 Louisa W.   And six others.

152

LUCY BROADDUS married WM. FURGUSON.

Twelve children, four living in 1888.

153

MARIA BROADDUS married JOHN S. WALLIS.

Children—252 Sarah.
           Thomas O.
       253 Mildred.
           Mary Russell.

155

CATHARINE BROADDUS married THOMAS W. BUTTS.

Children—   Ann E.
              Ellen N.
              James M.
              Martha F.
              Juliet A.
              Thomas E.
              Sarah C.

157

SARAH BROADDUS married JAMES BURDETT.

Children—   James B.
              Susan.
              Crawford.

159

JAMES G. BROADDUS married ELIZABETH S. GAINES.

Children—   Lucy.
              Ellen C.
              Elizabeth F.
              James Henry.
       254 Susan J.
       255 Sally J.

160

SUSAN C. BROADDUS **married** FREDERICK BURDETT.

Children—256 Sarah A.
           257 Columbia F.
                Martha C.
                Selina S.

164

REUBEN BROADDUS **married** MARTHA L. OLIVER.

Children—   William L.
           258 Robert B.
           259 John F.
                Reuben.
           260 Andrew.
           261 Willentina.
           262 Martha E.
           263 Jennie R.
                Mary E.
                Kate E.

165

EDWIN BROADDUS **married** ELIZA MONTAGUE.

Children—264 Muscal.
           265 William.
           266 Virginia.
                Bettie.

170

BETSY BROADDUS **married** Mr. ROBBINS

Children—   Broaddus.
                Albert.
                Lalla.
                Belle.

SIXTH GENERATION.

173

MARTHA BROADDUS **married** EDMUND SALE.

Children—   Judson.
                William.
                Alma.

174

JOHN BROADDUS married LAURA MOTLEY. (1st wife).
LUCY GOLDEN. (2nd wife).

175

SILAS B. BROADDUS married SALLIE GOLDEN.
Seven children.

178

SILAS J. GOLDEN married SUSAN PARKER.

Children—   John.
Silas.
Wilton.
Louis.
Molly.

.179

THOMAS W. GOLDEN married LOUIS REDD.

Children—   John.
Robby.
Worley.
Edmonia.
Lucy.
Georgia.
Molly.
Sally.
Nelly.

182

J. FRANK GOLDEN married VICTORIA MOTLEY.

Children—   Jack.
Burnley.

Miss VIRGINIA GREEN. (2nd wife).

Children—   Robie.
Myrtle.

Miss VIRGINIA TALLEY. (3rd wife).

Children—   Williamson.

184

LAVINIA GOLDEN married W. S. WHITE.

Children—   George.
Jack.
William.
Andrew.
Nannie.
Mattie.
Callie.

187

BETTY GOLDEN married Mr. CONWAY.

Children—   Lizzie.
James.
Coleman.
Powhatan.
Lysander.
Eustace.

196

ANDREW BROADDUS married GRACIE ASKIN.

Children—   John E.
Green B.
267 Jeremiah.
Andrew W.
William F.
Sidney C.
268 Elbridge J.
Mary.
Margaret.
Elizabeth.

200

WM. W. BROADDUS married Miss MOTLEY.

Children—   L cy.
Wallie.
Woodson, and others.

203

SARAH BROADDUS married Dr. ALSOP.

204

RICHARD F. BROADDUS married Miss VIRGINIA M. HENSHAW.

Children—269 Maurice E.
Willie R.
Manley.
Effie V.
Lucy.
Maxie G.
Richard Frank.

205

GEORGE W. BROADDUS married Miss HOCKER.

Children— Nicholas H.
Henry C.
James R.
W. Andrew.
Thomas M.

Married Miss HUNT. (2nd wife.)

Children— Kate.
John.
Simeon.
Clifton.
George
Elizabeth.

207

ELIJAH BROADDUS married MARTHA A. BROADDUS.

Children— Edward E.
James W.

208

JOSEPH E. BROADDUS married SARAH J. MOORE.

Children—   Thomas N.
           Elijah B.

Married Miss HARRIET WHITTAKER. (2nd wife.)

Children—   Harvey.
           Joseph.
           Mary J.
           Algernon.
           Martha J.
           Lue Jackson.
           George E.
           William D.

210

WM. J. BROADDUS married MARGARET E. CARTER.

Children—   William B.
           Charles M.
           Richard S.
           Robert B.
           Edward N.
           Sallie A.
           Mary L.
270   John F.

211

RICHARD S. BROADDUS married MARY J. CARTER.

Children—   Carter L.
           Jeannie.

214

JOHN L. MOTLEY married MARIA BROADDUS,

Children—   Cora.
           Laura.
           John.
           William.
           Tillie.
           Alice.
           Andrew.

218
REUBEN B. RICHARDSON.

Children—   William.
Frank.
Thomas H.
James R.
Nannie.

226

RICHARD H. BROADDUS married SARAH A. SANDERS.

Children—   Keziah.

227

JULIAN BROADDUS married HALLIE TERRELL.

Children—   Alford.
Gwinn.
Florence.
Louis
Andrew.
Hallie.
Carlisle.
Luther.
Howard

228

LUTHER BROADDUS married SALLIE E. BRYAN.

Children—   Aileen.
Lenore.

229

FLORENCE BROADDUS married Mr. WILLIAMS.

Children—   Jane E.

230

ANDREW BROADDUS married Miss ———.

Children—   Gay.
Carrie.
Lois.

231

EVELYN MONTAGUE married X. X. CHARTERS.

Children—   Florence.

232

ANDREW P. MONTAGUE married MAY CHRISTIAN.
Two Children.

233

RICHARD W. THOMPSON married HARRIETT GORDON.

Children—   Mary G.
Frederick F.
Richard W.
Charles.
Harry.
Virginia.

234

MARY J. THOMPSON married ANTHONY ADDISON.

Children—   John F.
Sarah.
Catharine.
Mary M.
Murray.
Olidia.
Keturah G.
Arthur D.
Anthony C.

235

MARTHA F. THOMPSON married SAMUEL CAMPBELL.

Children—   Martha F.
Mary C.
Antoinette A.
Phil. S.
Robert F.

236

WM. MILLS THOMPSON married MARY J. PARKER.

Children—
Margaret.
Catharine.
John B.
William M.

240

JAMES M. BROADUS married ELLEN B. GAINES.

Children—271 Clarence L.
Mary M.
Edmund P.
William S.
Thomas A.

Married MARY C. LEWIS. (2nd wife.)

Children—
Edmund L.
John J.
Susan.
Rosalie M.
Reuben L. L.
William F.
John C. G.
Lucy C. M.

241

MARTHA A. BROADUS married EDWARD BICKERS.

Children—272 Ann Carter.
Sarah M.
John E
Carrie W.

242

CAROLINE M. BROADUS married Rev. W. A. WHITESCARVER.

243

JOHN ALBERT BROADUS married MARIA C. HARRISON.

    Children—   Eliza S.
         273 Anna H.
             Maria F.

     Miss CHARLOTTE E. SINCLAIR.   (2nd wife.)

    Children—   Samuel S.
             Caroline.
             Alice B.
             Ella T.
             Boyce.

244

EDMUND S. BROADDUS married BETTIE A. BAKER.

    Children—   F. Webb.
             Mary E.
             William A.
             Willie C.
             Edmund S.
             Thomas P.

245

AMANDA F. BROADDUS married JOHN KEEN.

    Children—   Mary E.
             George B.
             Crawfordella.
             Martha L.
             John S.
             Nannie B.
             John W.
             Thomas.
             Charles F.

246

WM. H. C. BROADDUS married ANN DUDLEY.

    Children—   Willie Crawford.

247

MARY LOUISA BROADDUS **married** FRANCIS WEBB.

Children—   Crawford B.
     Mary F.
     Lucy W.
     Nannie S.
     Frank.
     Kate T.
     Mosely H.
     Charlton.
     Bessie May.

248.

THOMAS E. BROADDUS **married** KATE GAINES MAHAN.

Children—   Paul.

254

SUSAN J. BROADDUS **married** RICHARD STONE.

Children—   Lucy B.
     Richard T.
     James H.
     Mary C.
     Ellen B.
     John.

255

SALLIE J. BROADDUS **married** Rev. WM. STRINGFELLOW.

Children—   Ann.
     Richard.
     Susan B.
     James B.
     Lucy A.
     Robert.
     Eliza.
     Bruce W.
     Sallie R.

256

SARAH A. BURDETT married JOHN V. MARTIN.

Children— Frederick T.
Marian K.
Jessie B.
Elizabeth B.
Bedwood L.
Arthur G.

257

COLUMBIA F. BURDETT married ANDREW J. STONE.

Children— Mary F.
Martha B.
Lizzie H.
Florence B.
Ida B.

258

ROBERT BRUCE BROADDUS married HARRIET J. WILSON.

Children— Roddie.
Emma.
Lina.
Addie.

259

JOHN F. BROADDUS married ADIEN RIGGS.

Children— Charles.

260

ANDREW BROADDUS married MARY A. SMITH.

Children— Mortimer.
Robert B.
Russell.
Logan A.
Jesse.

261

WILLENTINA BROADDUS **married** CHARLES BODEKER.

Children— Edwin B.
Fannie B.
Nellie.

263

JENNIE R. BROADDUS **married** Dr. D. B. MILLER

Children— Reuben B.
Clifford M.

264

MUSCAL BROADDUS **married Miss** ANNIE MOUNTCASTLE.

Children— Annie.
Myrtle.

265

WILLIAM BROADDUS **married** SUSAN BOONE.

Children— Willow.
Elmore.

266

VIRGINIA BROADDUS **married** WILLIAM D. JONES.

Children— Edwin B.
Eliza.

267

JEREMIAH BROADDUS **married** JULIET OLDHAM.

Children— Andrew J.
William O.
Susan A.
Mattie.
Elbridge C.
Jerry.
Gracie.
Etta.
Eva.
Lizzie.
Lycurgus.

268

ELBRIDGE J. BROADDUS **married Miss** ——.
Children—   Joseph.

269

MAURICE E. BROADDUS **married** LILLIE R. CALDWELL.
Children—   Mary V.
Lucy H.
Maurice E.
Edna C.
Robert C.

271

CLARENCE L. BROADDUS **married** SARAH KEMP.
Children—   Thomas M.
Ellen B.

272

ANN C. BICKERS **married** JOHN M. FARRAR.
Children—   William E.
James M. B.
Thomas L.
John A.
Martha L.
Howard M.
Mercer G.

273

ANN H. BROADUS **married** W. Y. ABRAHAM.
Children—   John B.

www.ingramcontent.com/pod-product-compliance
Lightning Source LLC
Chambersburg PA
CBHW060451280326
41933CB00014B/2727